The Growing Crisis of Democracy Decline

'My vote won't change anything!'

Malcolm Plumb

Grosvenor House
Publishing Limited

This book is published by
Grosvenor House Publishing Ltd
Link House
140 The Broadway, Tolworth, Surrey, KT6 7HT.
www.grosvenorhousepublishing.co.uk

A CIP record for this book
is available from the British Library

ISBN 978-1-80381-609-8

Introduction

Malcolm F Plumb

This book is intended to be, mainly, of interest to one person and one person only. It is the voter attending polling stations for every type of election, both for local and national governments, and very occasionally when public referendums are held. BUT this book is particularly intended as a message to the non-voter, for reasons which will become clear in later chapters, estimated at 15 MILLION (about one third) for the most recent UK general election, 2019. It is written by an ordinary citizen ('floating') voter, who originally had no specialist, professional or academic knowledge in the subject of democracy and governmental systems. It is written specifically for the 'ordinary citizen', like me, who is not normally aware of 'inconvenient truths' of our very flawed system of democracy, which are intentionally hidden from view. The fundamental purpose in 'voting' is to enable all people to express their view upon how they wish to be governed, by whom and what they want in the future. This book is certainly NOT written for the benefit of any political party, or for the media or for anyone who holds power and influence in public policy matters or national issues. These include banks, public officials, politicians, the commercial world, religious, military, or other kinds of a nations 'people leaders'. These, I will repeatedly refer to as 'the elite' for reasons solely of word economy, not in any way, related to the 'complimentary' interpretations of this word.

As mentioned, the book's subject deals with matters about which I had little academic or professional knowledge, which has proved quite helpful! Why? I had no preconceived notions. What I did have is firstly a deep, long-standing impression that, somehow, 'ordinary' people (no offence!) are being collectively ignored, denied full information, abused, lied to and exploited without their knowledge or consent within the UK and other nations. And it also 'seemed' to me that there are substantially increasing reports that democracy is seriously being undermined. These doubts have their origins from my long (over 60 years) past working life in various roles for several kinds of local public bodies followed by two years' research from many reputable sources. I recall one particular incident from a comment made to me in private, many years ago by an honest and respected local councillor who had suddenly totally changed his stance upon a major council policy matter, upon which he had been very adamant. His comment to me, in private, was, 'For many in politics these days "objective one" is to stay in power, by foul means or fair'! Consequently, I now need to investigate this fear. Secondly, from different occupations and studies in management theory and practice, I am familiar with techniques of detailed research and writing essays and papers on particular subjects. However, when I began work, I also felt that my fears (summed up in the book's 'second' title) were going to be quite difficult to justify. How wrong could I have been! If anyone takes the trouble to carry out their own constructive and careful research, ignoring what many (not all) politicians, the 'media' and the 'elite' levels in society are saying, they too will find, as I have, an enormous amount of very worrying facts and authentic information, which has been kept out of the public eye. Not giving these facts with reasonable prominence is a public scandal. My initial view prompted me to research extensively from reliable sources of information, lest I include something that is totally unjustified. This work showed that my initial reaction/ fear was totally justified and created, for me this book's titles. I recall reading a book some time ago, about a naval battle during the First World War (the sea battle of Jutland). There is some debate upon who won this naval engagement, the British fleet or the German fleet. Admiral Jellico was the British naval commander. His famous comment after reviewing the losses of so many British ships, was along the lines of 'there is something bloody wrong with our ships today'. The 'something' he was referring to, turned out to be insufficient defensive armour plating against enemy shelling. I am adapting that famous understatement by substituting 'ships' for 'democracy'!

There is another somewhat less well-known saying. It is this. 'The people of England deceive themselves when they fancy they are free; they are so, in fact, only during the election of members of Parliament. But as soon as a new Parliament is elected, they are again in chains and are nothing'. Strong words, written in a paper 'The Social Contract' by Jean-Jacques Rousseau— in 1762! Are we heading back to that time? Or have we always been in this situation, AND it is worsening!

In my research, I have found that there is substantial and clear evidence of a growing distrust of politics, Parliament, and democracy, in an increasing percentage of the nation's people (as is part evidenced by the GROWING proportion of 'non-voters'), from many different sources and the many, many, publications on this very subject. A friend of mine who has officiated at 'vote counting' at Parliamentary elections told me of one case of a 'spoilt' (rejected) ballot paper. This voter had put a line across all the candidates' names with the words 'none of these' and added the comment '*Come back to life, Guy Fawkes. ALL is forgiven!*' I do not, of course, advocate doing what Mr Fawkes was attempting. But I do hope that responsible, effective and non-illegal action by the people will, very soon, restore a much higher level of true democracy in the very near future.

It might seem strange that despite the title of this book, I should include a 'claimed' acknowledgement of the current state of the UK's democracy. Reference is made to a recent 'democracy league table' of all the nations of the world (given as 180 in number). The UK ranks as 12th in this list (down from ninth). You may think 'well, that's not bad'. But it is 'bad', because we have dropped out of the single figure level. This is not the way we want to go. According to another survey published in a UK national newspaper (January 2020, entitled 'Democratic deficient'), the proportion of people who are dissatisfied with the state of democracy has reached its highest level on record, research has suggested, compared to the year 1990. In the UK, this level of dissatisfaction has increased from 38% of the population (1990) to about 60% (2020). 26 named nations have increased satisfaction and 21 have increased dissatisfaction. The worst case is the USA, being 52% (2020) compared to 24% in 1990 The UK now has about 58% 'dissatisfied' compared to 38% in 1990.

My research concentrated on three main characteristics of 'democracy'. Firstly, what is the universally accepted interpretation of this word? Secondly, what circumstances arise, currently, to either justify the book's title or to dispute it? This includes mainly the UK, the EU, but also other 'democratic' countries, and (most worryingly), countries where democracy simply does not exist. Thirdly, if the book's title is justified, what are the ways by which democracy might be restored, developed and improved to the benefit of the nation's majority (rather than the minority), and perhaps to the whole world generally?

My research has included recorded historical interpretations and conventions defining the word 'democracy', references to books written by well-respected, and knowledgeable authors who support the view that democracy is failing, the media (newspapers, the web, TV etc.) and current events. To these areas I have added my own personal opinions, comments and questions, and, to some extent, what happens in other countries and their impact upon their populations.

So far as the media 'press' are concerned, it has proved impossible to read every national morning paper, daily over a two-year long period, so I have limited my reading to just three newspapers which, in my own opinion, all satisfied five criteria:

- News reports of direct relevance to this book's title, backed up by responsible 'evidence'.
- Comments, observations and criticisms evenly distributed, politically.
- Political parties, pressure groups, religions or direct commercial, little evidence of excessive bias towards these organisations.
- Full adoption of professional conventions for media/ press standards, i.e., 'The Independent Press Standards organisation's rules and regulations, editors code of practice'.
- Clarity in writing and communicating.

The three newspapers I have used are the *Independent*. the *Times*, and the *Guardian*. This implies no criticism of all the remaining newspapers whatsoever. Subject to applying the minimum standards, they guarantee fulfilment of one essential condition of democracy, that is 'press freedom'. (I should also at this point declare I have no financial or other interests in any news media whatsoever).

Many very talented authors have questioned the declining level of democracy. I enter this vitally important area, as an ordinary (somewhat ill-informed) member of the public, to look at these claims through my eyes as a citizen/voter, to see if they make sense to an average, wholly independent 'floating' voter. I have found that the claims they make are well justified and that this is a very serious matter in today's world. I implore my readers to take every action they can (within the law) to demand an urgent, wholly independent, professional, people's investigation into the declining lack of true democracy, followed by a national referendum arranged and managed by a non-political people's assembly. This would be followed by an unreserved requirement to government to introduce the people's decision within a specified short period of time without any change to the people's referendum decision whatsoever. 'Democracy' has an increasingly serious problem of legitimacy if citizens no longer wish to take part in its most important element of going to the polling stations at elections. If the 'non-voters' totals continue to increase, how can it be claimed the government represents the nation's people?

Finally, I would like to express my unreserved appreciation to those authors of the books I have quoted. Do please put them (and others with similar titles) on your reading list. They are all well researched, non-political and completely independent. I could not have been given the enormous amount of information and facts to justify this book's title without their knowledge and wisdom. I must repeat that I have no financial interests whatsoever in applauding their work. They all tell the 'truisms' that you and I are progressively being denied. The extracts I have used from the media have proved extremely helpful and I strongly recommend much more reading of all the national daily papers. Be mindful, that they can be editorially and politically influenced, and they have an insatiable thirst for 'sensationalism' rather than what is a 'normal' state or position, but this has to be acceptable in a 'free' society. You can make your own judgements on that score. I pay tribute to the UK Electoral Reform Society for a wealth of factual information upon the state of our democracy. Again, go on their website and read their reports and items and you will begin to see the developing seriousness of the current situation. And finally, I applaud the increasing numbers of demonstrators who 'get off their arses' and try to influence governments to listen to the people. You may not agree with all that they argue for, but they are exercising their right to demonstrate and to communicate their views to the government. (You should see what happens in some other countries when this kind of action is taken!) As will be argued in later chapters, their rights to responsibly demonstrate is a fundamental principal for democracy!

This growing decline in democracy urgently needs 'nipping in the bud' before it gets worse. Only we, the people, can do this.

Contents

What Is Meant by 'Democracy?'

Before examining the effectiveness of any system or activity, we must begin by defining exactly what standards and conditions are required before we can say the 'system' or activity is 'satisfactory'—or otherwise. What, therefore, is meant by 'democracy'?

'Democracy' is a single word that answers the fundamental question in human society 'who rules?' The fairest answer is simply enough 'the people rule'. The problem is that this simple answer can mean anything to anyone. This means that politicians, governments, dictators can claim to be 'democratic' according to their own criteria and interpretation. Consequently, even in the 'developed' world, the wishes of the people can be easily ignored, and action taken which is wholly 'undemocratic'. In this scenario the real (hidden) 'objective number one' of this is,the pursuit, advancement and retention of personal power by 'an elite few', be they political, military, the world's (few) extremely rich, religions or just dictatorial leaders, rather than what the people think and want.

Historically, the basis of democracy originates from ancient Greece, the key (Grecian) words being 'cracy' meaning 'power' and 'demos' being 'the people'. Hence, this leads onto the simple definition of 'rule by the people'. However, there are increasingly, different definitions of democracy. Abraham Lincoln at the time of the American Civil War in emphasising the value and importance of democracy, gave his famous definition as 'government of the people, by the people and for the people'. The key words being, 'by', 'for' and 'of'. Two other definitions arise for democracy which underpins the problem in the original Athenian (Greek) term. These are 'direct' democracy and 'indirect' democracy. In the case of direct democracy this involves the complete participation of all people (not just 'the elite') in the local cities and communities by regular public meetings open to all and by individual referendums. Historically, however, the fear was summed up by 'rule by the ignorant and unenlightened people'. That might have been so in ancient times, but it is not all that true in today's world. 'Indirect' democracy refers primarily to our present system of national government where elected representatives form a government with the power to make decisions on behalf of the people. To do this, representatives must know what the people's wishes are. This arrangement has to my own mind, now serious limitations which will be discussed later in this book.

'Collins Dictionary' definition records that democracy means 'government by the people or their elected representatives', and 'favouring popular rights'. The definition of 'representative' means 'stand for', 'deputies for', 'act for', 'serve as', 'speak for' and 'assume the role of'. Two key features have always thus been accepted in the process of 'representation'. The first being that (in some way), a 'popular assembly' occurs, in which ordinary citizens debated and decided issues and policies for their society including important matters such as war and peace. The second feature involved the regular rotation of citizens, in turn, selected by 'lot' to serve on an executive (government) body. Hence the word 'representation' comes into play.

'Fascism' is the opposite of democracy. Dictionary definitions describe 'fascism' as an authoritarian political system opposed to democracy and liberalism. It is based upon the fascist doctrine of the totalitarianism state 'everything for the state, nothing against the state and nothing outside the state' involving the absorption of the individual in the community and obliterating any trace of individual identity. The problem with this 'doctrine' is the use of the word 'state'. Of the many dictionary definitions of this word, the most relevant is 'country', 'kingdom', and 'nation'. Is this not proof that fascism is completely undemocratic, because 'state' does not mean a 'dictatorial individual', or the 'elite few'. To my mind, this definition applies equally to both extreme 'capitalism' and extreme 'socialism' in the sense that all government actions are devolved to an elite few, again led by a dictatorial figure, in many areas of the world.

In the aftermath of World War Two, a universal declaration of human ('individual') rights was signed in 1948, which established democracy as a government system most supportive of individual rights. Article 21 (3) states 'The will of the people shall be the basis of the authority of government. This shall be expressed in periodic and genuine elections which shall be by universal and suffrage (right of voting) and shall be held in secret vote or by equivalent free voting procedures'. Despite there being a number of different interpretations of democracy, four main principals were defined by the US political scientist Larry Diamond and supported by a wide range of political institutions. The four elements were:

- Competition for power. The formation of political associations offering to the people different approaches/policies of government and governments being appointed following free and fair elections.
- Active participation of the people as citizens, in politics and civic life.
- Protection of fair and basic human rights.
- The rule of law, being applied equally to all citizens.

In David Beckham's excellent book, *Democracy: A beginners guide* (the circumstances of the many different approaches to defining democracy), David explains the differences for both 'democracy' (rule by the people etc.) and 'Oligarchy' (rule by the few). To quote these differences:

Democracy/Oligarchy

Public office open to all/Office restricted to those with special 'attributes' or 'qualifications'.

Selection to office by election/Selection by 'appointment'.

Freedom of expression/media/Censorship/controlled media.

Access to official information/Public office protected by secrecy.

Free 'associational life'/Association, a privilege.

Channels of upward influence/Communications only downwards.

Direct vote on constitutional change decided/Change only by an 'elite'.

Rights enforced by independent judges/Subordinate to judge's government.

What worries me a little by these definitions of 'democracy' and 'oligarchy' is that there is a very wide gulf between the two extremes. The aspect of 'representativeness' which is vitally important when judging the level of democracy within a nation is a most important element. The historical Greek notion, Abraham Lincoln's definition and dictionary interpretations all refer to 'the people'. 'people' means all persons generally, communities, human beings, citizens and so on. 'Representativeness' must therefore apply to all people. If 'democracy' precludes a government representing solely, specific 'elites', 'commercial interests', 'religions' or 'donors to political parties' and the like, I believe this factor could be added to the above list with appropriately worded descriptions for both columns.

At this point, one might ask why is it that so much emphasise is given in the interpretation to 'people' involvement, particularly when human beings are so advanced. Who needs people when we have so much technology? It is not too difficult, in my view, to see why. It is because of the enormous collective number of human talents, knowledge and experience, their likes, dislikes, reasoned thoughts, compassion, emotions, and 'front line' knowledge' of the nations needs and problems, i.e., 'their collective wisdom'. The list is endless. We will see in a later chapter how the increasing reliance upon information technology is becoming dangerous and serious.

The dictionary representation in democracy, does not, of course, define the processes involved. To my mind it means firstly understanding the views, feelings, wishes, fears, dislikes, hopes and needs and problems of all people in a nation. Having then established that (which is not in my opinion a major problem: elections, referendums, people's surveys, people's consultation etc.), it is to work to meet as many of those needs and wishes that are obtainable, strongly supported, fair and just, without creating new problems for the nation generally (e.g., Bankruptcy).

So, developing this theme further, there are basic concepts identified, which establish key concepts of democracy and provide more measures of 'representativeness'. They are:

- Acceptance of the principle that all people have different interests affected within a 'collective decision'.
- Every adult person is assumed to be capable of having a view upon matters of public interest.
- The best collective decision in an election/referendum are those where the people have full access to all relevant factors and truths with NO relevant truths hidden from view, or distortions and exaggerations of the truth.
- Where a single outcome cannot be agreed by any government representative body, upon vitally important national issues, the matter is referred to all people involved with, again, full unrestricted access to all relevant information. The circumstances

of applying this rule would be determined by a non-political, impartial, independent professional body.

- The principal of 'one person, one vote' regardless of background, position, gender, religion etc. ensures that every person is of equal worth.
- By voting in an election or a referendum, acceptance of the result ('the consensus view') is accepted by all people (and supported), unless fully justified challenges are made under previously specified grounds.
- 'Public accountability' means that those entrusted with all forms of government have a duty to be able to explain and justify their ('representative') actions and the use of public money, paid by the people. This should be enshrined by the law.

Of all the different elements of what we understand to be the current conventions of what is meant by 'democracy', it seems to me that they are all in need of recognising the reality of 'today's state' of the modern world. Mankind has moved on by considerable strides since all the historical definitions of democracy. Firstly, we have the tremendous advances in scientific knowledge and information technology. This factor alone should enable ALL people to be able to be involved in providing consensus views of their wishes and expectations. Again, this should be enshrined by legal statute which forbids the hiding of relevant, accurate and verifiable information from the public eye. This condition is NOT unreasonable and can be verified as justice and fair play, by later examples quoted in this book. In a later chapter we consider how 'information' increases 'personal power', when kept secret from 'the many' and thereby decreases democracy levels. Secondly, mankind has—sadly—developed many awful weapons of mass destruction which can be used by undemocratic, dictatorships, who simply possess these weapons for one purpose only. To retain and, if possible, to extend their own 'power' base. Thirdly, we continue to see what to my mind is increasing examples of cruel, wholly unjust examples of dictatorial rule in many countries resulting in increasing incidences of mass refugee migrations. Put together two simple facts, being (a) cruel and wholly unjust dictators in 'underdeveloped' nations (and others!), and (b) their increasing access to weapons of mass destruction. We must accept the claim that mankind has already reached the stage of total planetary destruction. The current interpretations of 'democracy' then urgently needs to be strengthened and updated and (I am afraid) the introduction of worldwide enforcements for all nations to meet at least the important basics of democratic rule. By way of example only (acting as just an 'ordinary citizen'), in any country, my views are that firstly, it should be the unrestricted right of all peoples in all nations to have unrestricted access to specified information upon their own government's actions. Secondly scientific research must be 'policed' and monitored professionally and independently to a much greater extent. The task of true science is NOT to provide new weapons or scientific advances which gives considerable benefit for the world's 'elite', to enforce and increase their influence and personal power. It is to defend and advance our beautiful world, its people, its environment and all aspects of it. There are other proposals which, again as an ordinary citizen, seem to be urgently needed and these will be discussed in the final pages. For now, I am simply saying this: 'democracy' interpretations have to be updated and accepted by a new worldwide convention and then positive action has to be taken to increase all nations' abilities to develop 'rule by the people'.

So, at this stage, I hope we have a basic understanding of the important elements of democracy, which enables us 'the citizens', to have a 'yardstick' against which we can measure both democratic standards and the level of 'representativeness'.

* * *

The Present-day Government Structure in the UK

With apologies to those of my readers who are considerably more knowledgeable and experienced in this area than I am, it must be accepted that many 'ordinary' citizens (like me!), are not completely clear upon who does what in the UK Government and how. I suspect that this lack of awareness is one factor for the growing apathy towards the government generally which again is seriously worrying. Also, with a book of this title, it must, in my view, have some reference to the UK's government 'system' currently in force which is the subject under review. So, here is the 'briefest of the briefest' description of the UK Government's structure and tiers, extracted in part from the government's website 'Parliament UK', and from other sources.

- The UK national government structure comprises two separate 'Houses' in Westminster, London. The first is the House of Commons where elected members of Parliament debate and decide all kind of government policies and decisions and laws. 'MPs' are all elected by the people during four-yearly (or less) general elections. There are 650 constituencies throughout England, Northern Ireland, Scotland and Wales that form the 'United Kingdom'. The current electoral system for determining which political party 'rules' the governments activities, is called 'first past the post'. This simply means that the party which wins more than half of the 650 constituency 'seats', wins the election by 'majority' rules, and becomes the government. Whilst in theory the party winning 326 seats becomes the 'government', in practice, the party needs to win with a 'workable' majority (higher than 326) to cover for absences from government sessions, sickness and (often, these days!) members of the majority party who 'abstain' from voting or even vote against their own party. In this situation, the majority party either chooses to try to govern as a 'minority government' or negotiates with another political group to form a 'coalition' government to have a workable majority. As mentioned, it is solely the House of Commons which decides all the policies of the government elected and in power, and the actions and laws to be enforced. The House of Commons is referred to as the 'Lower House' (for historical reasons, today, that escapes me!). The problem with the current electoral system, in the minds of an increasing number of people, is that the system of 'first past the post' is seriously flawed and will always result in an 'unrepresentative' government of the people's needs and views. This is that in most, if not all, elections, more voters voted AGAINST having the particular political party in power, by voting for other political parties. Let us test this view against past, verifiable statistics. The following table shows the elections results of all elections since the Second World War (1945), extracted from the HM government's library website.

Year/Political party elected/Votes FOR/Votes AGAINST

1945 Labour 48% 52%
1950 Labour 46% 54%
1951 Conservative 48% 52%
1955 Conservative 50% 50%
1959 Conservative 50% 50%
1964 Labour 44% 56%
1966 Labour 48% 52%
1970 Conservative 46% 54%
1974 Labour (minority gov) 37% 62%
1974 Labour 40% 60%
1979 Conservative 44% 56%
1983 Conservative 42% 58%
1987 Conservative 42% 58%

1992 Conservative 42% 58%
1997 Labour 43% 57%
2001 Labour 41% 59%
2005 Labour 35% 65%
2017 Conservative (minority gov) 42% 58%
2019 Conservative 43% 57%

These accurate and verifiable facts show that in all election results since the end of the Second World War (1945) to 2019 (21 separate elections), more people voted against the incoming political party than for it. The 'worst' case was the 2005 general election where the Labour Party formed a 'minority' government, having received only 35% support of the total votes cast, with 65% against having a Labour government. The 'best' case was in 1955 where the vote was equal at 50% for, and 50% against. The second significant factor is that in all 21 separate elections since WWII the result was that either one of the two main political parties came into power. It is, quite clearly, an inescapable conclusion, that 'first past the post' guarantee's either the Conservative or the Labour Party will always win. It is difficult to avoid a question from a colleague of mine, 'is there perhaps an unpublished, unwritten secret, an unspoken understanding between the two main political parties to work against any other alternative of "first past the post election" principal?' Another saying that springs to my mind is 'divide and conquer'. Could this be another 'tactic' to keep one or the other of the two main parties in power? Also, on a side issue, is this not a case of (as someone once described it) 'seesaw politics', which creates a constant (and costly) reversion of the previous political party's policies and the introduction of 'new' ones?

In an article in the *Times* newspaper (August 2022), the full-page headline was 'Soaring bills, cold houses, blackout threat… where did it all go wrong?' Many failings are well defined. To my mind, however, the real reason is progressive, repeated 'not fit for purpose', seesaw politics by both Conservative and Labour governments since the end of the Second World War. The above statistics demonstrate the continuing mismanagement of the UK nation by wholly unrepresentative governments over a long period of time. The reality is at last coming out. The 'collective wisdom of the people' in NOT voting for the incoming government has been consistently RIGHT!

However, back to the election results given above. Another fact which is not immediately apparent is that the results clearly show the (rounded up/down) vote percentages for votes actually cast. It does not refer to the growing incidence of people not bothering to vote at all. Estimates vary on this, but a reasonable 'guestimate' would be in the order of one third of the total electors in the UK entitled to vote did not do so. For the 2019 general election, the HM gov. website confirms that the total number of people eligible to vote was 47,600,000 (rounded up figures). The total votes cast was 67.30%, with 33% (about one third) 'no votes'. According to my 'abacus bead frame', this means that 32 million voted, but 15 million did not. Of the wide percentage proportion of the 'non' voters, two considerations seem to me to be prevalent. Firstly, the wholly mistaken view that 'my vote will not change anything', and the increasing lack of trust by the people in politics and the government generally. From these presumptions, it is not unreasonable to conclude that a large proportion of the 'non-voters' was, and is, against the incoming government? Whatever the proportion is (we have no idea on this aspect), it is nevertheless a factor which increases, even further, the percentage of votes given in the table of all 24 general elections since the end of WWII, of voters who did not want the incoming governing political party. Consequently, it is an inescapable opinion that the 'elected' incoming government in all 24 elections did not represent the people's majority view. What better case do we have which justifies a complete overhaul of the current UK's undemocratic system. Is this not a 'sensational' subject for the attention of the media? If not, why not?

There are two other aspects of the UK's Electoral system, which must be questioned. Without going into yet another set of published statistics, it can be clearly shown that the ratio of votes between the 'main' political parties and the 'other' (no disrespect) political groups and parties in terms of Parliamentary seats obtained show a considerable variation. Put simply, candidates for election from 'other' parties collectively must get more votes to obtain one Parliament seat than the two main parties. Consequently, the views and wishes of ALL the voters, who voted for these 'fringe' (again, no disrespect) parties are not represented at all. Is this fair? Proof of this is, again, openly available on the HM gov. website 'total votes and seats for each party, for the 2019 general election' (This will be discussed further in the later chapter on 'democracy restoration').

Finally, one last 'problem' (which may well attract some protest) is the total number of groups registering themselves as 'political parties' and then putting up a candidate for election. If you look at the gov. website mentioned above ('total votes and seats etc.'), you will see a large list of 'specific interests' groups. In law, this is permitted. From this list you will see that the total number of 'parties' which stood for election but failed to get a single seat in the government was 58 separate parties out of the total of 68. And yet these parties attracted over 200,000 votes nationally, more than four other parties on the list, all of whom got Parliament seats. I do not argue, as some do, that this exceptionally large number of 'fringe' parties only serves to divert people's attention away from important national issues. However, I read somewhere that one (truly) democratic nation lays down, what I think, is a reasonable condition for these parties. It is that if a registered 'party' fails to achieve a minimum specified level of votes in an election, they are debarred from standing at the next election. A further condition, to my mind, is the parties who identify themselves as 'local issues'. The nation's Parliament deals with NATIONAL issues. LOCAL council elections deal with 'local' issues. These parties should be barred from standing, because voters already have several local candidates standing for their own constituency from the 'main' political parties. If these rules were applied, the national total of votes cast for all parties at general elections would be wholly regarding national issues only. Tactically, I can see that the main parties would oppose this change because it could seriously affect their own chances of being elected. (The rule 'divide and conquer' applies?)

Another aspect of 'representativeness' of the UK Government, concerns the published rules for all elected members of government. All members are required to act within an openly published 'code of conduct'. Section 3 of the code (part 6) states 'members shall have a duty to act in the interests of the nation as a whole, and a special duty to their constituents'. Question. Does this not mean 'self-interests', e.g., staying in power as an MP; party loyalty; taking time with other outside (well rewarded) activities; improving their party-political status etc. must never enter their minds, before the interests of the nation and their own constituents?

In a recent survey of people's TRUST in MPs representing the people's interests, it indicated a pronounced drop in their level of trust. More of this in a later chapter.

I hope you will allow me to be a little cynical by quoting another current news item (6th Feb. 2022). 'MPs back the banning of "glue traps" for... RATS!'. MPs gave their backing to the "Glue Traps (Offences) Bill" to make it an offence for the purpose of catching a rodent'. How about that for 'representing people's interests? Are you not impressed? How about making it an offence also for elderly people to die at a certain age, from malnutrition or being unable to obtain NHS care? Also, in respect of 'representing people's interests' a web news item (again Feb. 2022) tells us 'Home secretary is making one final push to criminalise (people's right) to protest (by demonstrations)'. To quote the actual wording of the report, 'The government has now confirmed that the "Policing Bill" comes back to the (House of) Commons, this month, fresh from a series of historic defeats in the House of Lords. Peers stripped it of some of the most egregious powers it contained. But it still has the ability to do what the home secretary always intended it to. It criminalises the right of (people) to protest'. (Definitely, in my view, another 'future' PEER for the House of Lords!)

Additionally, in relation to the 'representativeness' aspect of 'democracy', it is interesting to note that in the 'lower' levels of government structures in the UK (county, borough, town, parish councils) the representativeness element is much firmer. I quote from the code of conduct for a local borough council's website. This states that a councillor's role is 'Championing the needs of residents, the whole community, and in a special way, ALL constituents, including those who did not vote for you, putting their interests first.' ('One rule for one…')

We also should look at the question of 'referendums'. Again, the government's website tells us that referendums are a method of referring a question, or a set of questions to the entire electorate directly. Since 1973, there has been 11 referendums held in the UK, the majority of these related to the issue of devolutions. Wikipedia tells us that they are controlled by the Election and Referendums Act 2000 and the Parliamentary voting system and Constituencies Act 2011, but they are, by tradition, rarely used due to the principal of (preserving) 'Parliamentary sovereignty'. My perspective? National sovereignty is not a 'faultless' policy in any nation or society. There will always be issues which are just too important to leave to politicians in any democratic nation. All governments are prejudicial in respect of their beliefs and philosophies. If a government cannot decide a major issue, by a reasonable majority, over a specified period, and they choose not to have a general election, they should then be required, by statute, to hold a referendum, controlled and wholly managed by an independent, non-political, professional body, with a reasonable number of electors, selected by 'lot' from the whole UK. They would decide the wording of the question being put to the electorate and would issue an independent information paper which clearly defines facts and circumstance needed to assist the voters in making their choice. If political parties want to issue their own preferences, they should be free to do so.

There has been, of course, already a past referendum on the very subject of the current electoral system. This was the 2011 'Alternative Vote Referendum'. Following the 2010 general election, which resulted in a brief coalition government between the Conservative and Liberal parties, the question of the democratic representativeness of the 'first pass the post' concept was raised. It was agreed to give the electorate the choice of staying with the current system or applying an 'alternative voting system'. I remember this referendum, thinking at the time that voters were simply not being given enough information upon alternatives upon which to base their choice. Was this 'agreement' to hold a referendum, a condition of the Liberal party for joining the coalition government in power, I wonder? So, in the minds of the voters, the simple choice was, do we stick with the current system or change to 'something else' without any definition upon 'something else' whatever. How could anyone make their own judgement without knowing anything more about the alternatives? My view now? This was a blatantly 'politically engineered' referendum to ensure the current 'first past the post' system (guaranteeing election of only either one of the two main parties) would continue. How could anyone vote for 'something else'? We need this referendum again, this time organised by an independent, non-political group made up of a combination of experts in appropriate disciplines, the Electoral Reform Society, and a 'jury' of people 'citizens'. Result of this 'referendum'? A very low turnout of electors was the result (just 42% nationally), with voters probably taking the line 'better the devil you know'.

- Another 'method' of defending the 'claim' of high democratic levels is to offer people the opportunity to organise petitions either FOR a new public policy or AGAINST a government policy. I gather that if a petition acquires more than 10,000 signatories, the government MUST issue a response. Big deal! All the government has to do is to issue some political excuse for not accepting the petition! Job done, move on, no right of appeal.
- The other House is the House of Lords, where all members (called 'peers') are appointed by the nation's sovereign, currently the king, but on the advice of the nation's prime minister. The majority of appointees come from the four main political parties. A few non-political members are recommended by an independent body, 'The House of Lords

Appointment Commission'. 'Life' peers (currently 661) are appointed for the whole life of the appointee. Other peers, called 'excepted hereditary peers' (currently 91) now also remain for life, but the former 'hereditary' element (the peerage being passed on automatically to the next generation) is withdrawn following the House of Lords Act 1999. The remaining numbers comprise 26 bishops, creating a final total of 778. The House of Lords no longer holds any real 'power' of government in making actual governmental decisions. Their functions are 'to debate the House of Commons policies and government decisions; formally to question such policies and decisions; to put forward proposed changes to bills (draft legislation); and to propose private members bills'. However, the final word always rests entirely with the House of Commons.

To summarise their 'official' role, the House of Lords, 'using their professional experience and specialist knowledge' assists in making effective laws, hold government (the House Commons) to account, and to investigate public policy.

Members of the House of Lords can claim up to £300 each day for attendance, plus travelling and other expenses. However, in one fairly recent (critical) perspective of the income actually being paid to peers, the *Evening Standard* news website (October 2017) claimed 'that 115 Lords claimed nearly £1.3 million in the past year despite not speaking once in the 'Upper' chamber, and that 17 Lords pocketed £424,637 in expenses between them in the past year despite failing to speak, sit on a committee or submit a written question'. These and other aspects are causing increasing concern in many sections of society and will be discussed further in the final chapter 'Restoring Democracy Actions'. There are growing views that the 'Upper House' appointments system itself is extremely flawed and prejudiced. It is said that appointments are only given as a reward for past services to the wellbeing of the nominating political leader/party, or as a promise to internal political party MP's to maintain support for the party's leadership, and that appointments are made with the intention of increasing political influence within the House of Lords. In an article in a national, *Independent* newspaper (August 2022), the 'outgoing' prime minister's honours list (to the House of Lords) is openly criticised as 'scandalous', quoting comments from a well-respected former government standards chief

A somewhat more outrageous view is that some appointments are offered to those whom the party want to remove from positions of influence within the party itself. (NO, surely not! This kind of action would never happen?!) Really? Front-page headline, 5/6 February 2022 '(Boris) Johnson (UK prime minister) offering peerages and knighthoods to try to win ("personal"?)

support'. Once again, whose money would he be spending if he was successful? And, again, to be fair, I should quote another MP from the ruling party, who had the bottle to admit, 'PM is too busy seeing off threats (against him) to govern'.

It would be fair to accept that some of the 'peers' do provide some form of 'auditing' of the actions of the House of Commons. But, as mentioned already, there are signs beginning to emerge that in addition to the claim that the real levels functionality of the 'Upper House' are exceedingly low (political/financial loyalties), 'peers' themselves are becoming so alarmed at current levels of government corruption to even contemplate giving up their very lavish style of living. Evidence of this? An article in the *Evening Standard* (March 2022) headed 'Minister (in the Upper House) says fraud in the government is "rampant" after a dramatic resignation'. This report states that a minister in the 'Upper House' (House of Lords) had quit after criticising the 'Lower House' (House of Commons) for 'Schoolboy level swindling' of fraudulent Covid business loans. He claimed (the report states) 'that the government had failed spectacularly for allowing dysfunctionality to continue on such a colossal scale'. The article goes on to say that the level of fraud in government is rampant. Public estimates sit at just under £30bn. Annually!

Levelling up policy with the nation's real wealth creators (as defined earlier) and 'levelling down policy' from the government fraudsters? Bring it on! (This aspect will be referred to later.)

However, I cannot again resist the temptation to quote two very different rules which apply in the ('presumed') Upper House, regarded by many as the 'highest' level of the UK Government, to the rules which apply to the 'lowest' levels of government (county, borough, town and parish). We note that 'lords' hold their ('appointed') positions for life (even if they do not attend meetings, etc.) and receive a grotesquely high level of income. At the 'lower' levels of government, councillors HAVE to get elected by their constituents, receive little allowance (or, in respect of 'local' councils, town, parish, no allowances at all), and, if they fail to attend a meeting for a period of six months, are automatically, by law, 'sacked' from the council (i.e., 'lose' their seats). Also, it is an absolute requirement that when a matter comes up for discussion, local councillors MUST declare an interest in ANY connection with 'outside interests' directly or indirectly related to an item being debated upon council business. Again, failure to do so could result in serious level of censure for even a minor matter.

However, on the subject of 'conflicting standards of conduct' between the 'lowest' and 'highest' levels of government, we see more examples of serious differences in standards. In an article in the *Guardian* newspaper (August 2022) we read 'a hereditary peer' (non-appointed peer who automatically inherits his peerage from his parents, on their death) is under investigation for the second time by the 'House of Lords Standing Watchdog Committee over allegations that he misused his Parliamentary position to lobby for a firm that was paying him as a "Consultant". He apparently did this by "tabling" nine questions for specific government information, and then passed this onto the company concerned, presumably (?) to provide some form of commercial advantage (?)." Let us hope and pray this is an isolated case!

My perspective? The House of Lords is NOT a people's representative body and needs substantial electoral reform, or complete replacement (as discussed in greater details later). The House of Lords is 100% 'not fit for purpose' (and bloody expensive!). It should be replaced, in a way decided by the people with, say, a 'people's assembly' chosen regularly by 'lot' (similar to the law courts jury system) supported and advised by non-political, independent professional advisers from relevant disciplines.

Freedom of the Press:
The Positives and the Negatives

Firstly, from the outset, I would like to clarify one vitally important aspect concerning the roles and activities of the press and media in today's world. It is that, in accordance with one of the most critical elements of democracy, it is an absolute requirement, in any truly democratic nation, that the freedom of the press and media must be defended and preserved. 'Democracy' simply does not exist without this. What is my own personal perspective? I might not agree with some things which the press report and print. In some cases, I am horrified and quite angry with some wholly unjustified, prejudiced reports I see and read. But I will defend their right of press freedom absolutely. Throughout this book, I refer to the notion that information has a direct impact on power. This is particularly the case for 'the elite'. The more they have, the more power they can wield. They have access to a much wider source of facts and situations than we (the people) realise. But how much information is available to us, the people? The answer is considerably less. Therefore, our decisions at 'voting times' are based upon what we see (in our lives) and what we read. This second point is why – with certain conditions – it is essential for us, the people, to have high standards operated by the press and media, so that we can make more informed decisions at election times. In actually writing a book with this title, I am using my right to publicise my own perspective and views of the UK democracy and to express my opinions upon causes, improvements and remedies. Some of which I expect to be (partially at least) unjustified or genuinely impractical. These same rights must apply to the press and the media, despite political/editorial prejudicial press items, UK newspapers have proved to be an exceptionally useful source of true information in my research for this book. This must be acknowledged, without reservation.

However, every freedom has to have its own conditions and a reasonable level of restrictive control. We need to consider this aspect carefully before forming our own conclusions upon the benefits of press freedom, and the negative aspects of today's actions by the media. Somewhere I read a quote from a responsible and authoritative source. It was along the following lines. 'What a person sees, hears and reads often become reality to them. It affects their beliefs, opinions, attitudes and actions, often to a distorting extent'. I take the liberty of offering everyone a quote from Islam's Holy Prophet

Mohammed, given in the Holy Quran, which is: 'O ye who believe! If a wicked person comes to you with any news, first ascertain the truth, less Ye harm other people unwittingly and then become full of remorse for what Ye have done'. I, myself, am a Christian, with much respect for *almost* all other religions in our world and I commend this principal to all the faiths of the world. Similarly, in the Holy Bible (Christian), I recall an incident when Jesus Christ encountered a 'public stoning to death' incident. In this case, Jesus, held out a stone in his hand to the gathered crowd and said 'let he who is without sin, cast the first stone'. (Just one example of the many similarities between two of the largest and most influential religions of the world.) But let us try to understand the basic standards and a 'yardstick' by which we may make a judgement upon all forms of press and media in the UK and their influence upon people's views and opinions.

Firstly, let us look at one 'half' of the media, being radio and TV. I quote from the excellent legal website 'In Brief'. This site helps us to better understand various legal issues including the press and media, television and radio stations in the UK. The Office of Communications ('*Ofcom*') controls the statutory regulations of commercial television and radio stations, as well as the BBC, in the UK. 'Ofcom' also regulate video on demand and the airwaves over which 'wireless' devises operate. Since April 2017, Ofcom provides ethical rules which broadcasters must adhere to or face sanctions. Of particular relevance to the subject of this book is that 'broadcasters' must produce politically impartial comment, but this does not require them to be 'politically impartial' themselves. Ofcom's objective is to protect consumers and citizens from 'distortion' of the facts in order to manipulate the public's view of the news. This condition is SO IMPORTANT and we should all look for increased action to develop this standard in our society. It also seeks 'to protect from encouraging ANY form of violence or tension...' These are a vitally important principals (and 'yardsticks') for us to use in forming our own conclusions when listening and watching radio/TV broadcasts. How far do YOU feel Ofcom's objectives are being achieved?

Secondly, in respect of 'journalism' (all media newspapers and journals), and again quoting from 'In Brief', there is no statutory regulations for 'print' journalism. The exception being 'anti-monopoly legislation' (now there's an interesting new area to investigate!) and civil and criminal laws. So, how is 'freedom of the press' fairly regulated in this area? The answer is 'self-regulation', carried out by the Press Complaints Commission paid for by the printed newspaper and magazines companies themselves. The PCC Editors' 'code of practice' is the Commission's guide to ethics, and this is used to adjudicate complaints about newspaper content and the actions of journalists as part of their information acquisition work. (One wonders at this point, who controls the 'ethics' of the paparazzi?!). I am no lawyer, and I am confused that we have two existing laws, being Protection from Harassment Act 1997 and the Public Order Act 1986, which seem to me to be relevant in these cases but – seemingly – are never used in respect of the 'paparazzi'. The problem is that the PCC has no power to penalise breaches of the code or to impose sanctions in such cases. The deterrent element in cases of repeated infringements of the code may result in the newspaper involved dismissing the reporter concerned. However, it is fairly clear that this kind of control is somewhat effective because one often sees 'correction statements' published whenever a previous newspaper article has been shown to be incorrect or unjustified.

However, despite statutory controls and other standards laid down to control the excesses of the media, occasional wholly unjustified 'sensational' assertions are still published both nationally and internationally. Two examples illustrate this point. Firstly, the wholly unjustified police raid on the home of Sir Cliff Richard whilst he was away abroad, which was covered (would you believe!) by filming the raid from a private (media arranged?) helicopter! The reason for the raid, we were told was to obtain evidence of a form of criminal activity, which was wholly untrue, and this was later shown to be the case. The clear intention was trying to discredit the famous singer (in the pursuit of 'SENSATALISM') which failed completely. Secondly, the case of the wholly unjustified claims against the parents of the missing child

Madeleine McCann who was 'taken' by someone whilst on holiday with her parents. Again, those claims were wholly unjustified, but they both provided sensational (circulation increasing) 'scoops' for the media concerned.

Much more recently (2021), an incident occurred in the UK concerning fuel for road vehicles. A story was put out by a 'national newspaper', that a fuel shortage crisis was about to happen caused by a 'reduction' in the nation's fuel supplies. Result? As we all now know, miles of vehicles topping up at petrol stations throughout the UK, often causing traffic chaos. The truth was, as we now know, was there NO change in the supply level and availability of fuel stocks. But a crisis was created by people panicking (understandably) and buying up fuel far more than their normal needs. Was the newspaper ever 'brought to justice'? Not to my knowledge at least. AND did we not notice how fuel prices suddenly 'soared' during this incident? One result? Fuel sales increased substantially, at higher prices. What I would like to see, from an authoritative, independent source, is firstly the national fuel sales figures two months before the crisis and the average price being charged, compared with comparative figures during the months of the actual 'panic buying' period. We the people paid these prices. We the people have a right for an honest and full explanation.

Then we have clear examples of some newspapers blatantly trying to tell people how to vote at general elections (and the occasional referendum). It is not too difficult for us to recognise this type of newspaper activity. So long as measured, accurate and truthful arguments are put forward, few people would have any objection to this. One of the things I object to is when two national newspapers printed deeply offensive headlines against the successful political party who won the election. Right or wrong, that was the 'majority' decision of the voters under the current system of elections, and it should have been respected as such. The UK general election system is (in my view) seriously flawed (as is shown in a later chapter) but it is the only system we (the people) have at present and newspapers should never, by implication, aim their own views against the voters.

Another headline at this time was that democracy has been dragged into the dirt in this (general) election, because of distorted, deceptive and disruptive campaigning practices which are becoming increasingly normalised. Very true! By political parties and the media. Not by the voters who are using a flawed electoral system, who have been misled, lied to and denied access to the truth and facts and fed with unjustified claims. As the article rightly states, 'The quality of people's voting decisions is a direct function of the amount, completeness, accurate and relevant information available to them!' Another example of this situation (July 2022) following the then prime minister (at the time) finally resigning was reported in one of my 'selected' daily newspapers. Despite most of his own members opposing his leadership, the article confirmed 'The Tory press was with him to the death'. Blatant political propaganda!

Newspaper front-page headlines are often specifically worded in such a way to attract shock, scandal, concerns, even anger and thereby to increase more sales than rival newspapers. This is often by articles which are often prejudiced and omits contradictory truisms. Read these more carefully to consider the way they try to 'engineer' people's views and attitudes. Politicians who possess a 'talent' for this kind of action, often earn much more support, promotion AND later rewards.

Whenever I am suspicious that the media are trying to 'engineer' my opinions and views, I often go on the web, using keywords to get factual information upon claims and assertions from truly independent, professional sources. For example, in a later chapter in this book, in connection with the UK immigration problem ('Where Democracy is Either Non-existent...') I tested out a recent headline which claimed (rightly!) that one nation in Europe with a much greater land size (France) was accommodating far less immigrants than the UK. I found an up-to-date website which gave accurate figures for ALL nations in Europe which clearly showed that the ratio of land size to current population was, by far, the highest in the UK! Why was only France featured in the headline?

The unfortunate fact is that lies, distortions, rumours and exaggerations are far more popular/believable, and 'entertaining', than the actual truth of a situation, which can be 'boring' to the reader. I recall some years ago an advertisement for sausages! and the 'theme' of the advert was 'sell the sizzle, not the sausage'! (A good example of how 'politic speak' works!) In a later chapter we shall consider how the truth is often hidden from view for various reasons. We must remember that press freedom', despite being an essential condition of democracy, often has a strong 'commercial/profit/personal interests' aspect and motive. Sadly, the alternative is media totally controlled by the 'state'. (God forbid!)

One other 'political trick', which surprisingly does not appear to be noticed by voters. A few months before a general election, have you ever noticed that 'community aspects' (taxation, allowances, regional government grants etc.) suddenly become 'better'. Election takes place and a new government is created. Then after the election, we get told to 'tighten our belts' in order to make things better. Watch the headlines carefully both before the election and afterwards. Then test whether my impression is correct, or not.

To be fair, some newspapers have 'the balls' to accept the failings of the media. An article in a 'quality' newspaper in December 2019 headed 'how rival newspapers tried to tell (the voters) how to vote in this (2019) general election'. To his credit, the writer openly stated, 'The media (press) is becoming grotesquely, objectionably prejudiced, politically, during this election'. On behalf of the voting public, I say 'well said!' Thank you!

In yet another recent example, the web news quoted an extract from one of my own preferred newspapers concerning the UK's 'outgoing' prime minister in 2022. No less than four national daily newspaper were described as 'with him right to the very end'. I totally agreed. Blatant political propaganda!

On the credit side, however, at last, the truth about the growing, very serious danger of information technology is coming out about its effect upon WORLDWIDE democracy. The 'effect' being influencing people views and opinions and so controlling their actions without them realising it, undermining public policies, controlling public services, spying upon people again without them realising it, manipulating law and order, and even more 'empowering' the 'elite' classes of the whole world.

Think these claims are ridiculous? I pay particular tribute to one of my chosen UK morning newspapers, the *Guardian* for their front-page EXPLOSIVE (seven-page) article on 11 July 2022 upon, and I quote, 'How Silicon Valley tech company, flouted laws, duped police, exploited violence and aggressively lobbied governments during its GLOBAL expansion'. The front-page headline? 'The Uber files leak reveals secret lobbying operation to conquer the world'.

I have only been able to understand some parts of this seven-page article, prepared by a TEAM of experts, but it clearly demonstrate to me (one of the 'unwashed unclean and ignorant peoples'!) our vulnerabilities in these kind of circumstances. Please, please, read it, particularly if you have a high level of 'IT' skills and can better understand the extreme seriousness of this report better than I. You are better equipped to oppose this danger than I and many others. In the meantime, congratulations to the *Guardian* for their extensive investigational work. This article represents to me the best 'warning, truthful NEWS' I have seen in my research work.

I repeat, any freedom in a 'civilised' democratic nation must still have rules. The code of practice by the Press Complaint Commission (mentioned earlier) is simply not effective. It needs higher standards, legally defined and supported by independent lawyers. The unfortunate sad fact is that lies, distortions, rumours and exaggerations are far more popular, believable, 'entertaining' and 'profitable' in terms of circulation rates, than the actual truth (which can be 'boring' to readers).

What is my 'perspective' on this situation? Without resorting to regulations which substantially affects the basic democratic requirement for press freedom, I believe that at least two new standards should be added to our yardsticks. Firstly, an 'advisory yardstick'. This would require the inclusion of more verifiable facts to justify headline assertions. Quoting, for example, authoritative sources. This would also require the press to publish known, verifiably aspects, which are contrary to the viewpoint, emphasis or substance of the news item. In this case, if it can be shown that a newspaper knew of such contrary aspects beforehand, and failed to publish them, this should be regarded as 'intentional distortion' as defined by Ofcom's standards for radio/ TV quoted above, and, in my view, be brought before the courts for a 'jury' verdict. The newspaper should then be required to publish an appropriate admission in an equally prominent position to the original article (NOT in small print on page 23!). I would also suggest that there are strong grounds for the criminal laws to be activated (or amended) to provide additional protection against some of the dreadful harassment activities of the 'paparazzi'. Just one photograph of a well-known personality with a rare, odd expression on their face can earn a lot of 'dosh' from some of the paparazzi and media, but such a picture can and does affect people's views of the person involved!

It is, to my mind a little unrealistic in our modern world to expect readers to have to investigate whether what they are reading and seeing is fair, important and accurate. Newspapers should be more responsive to what the people want and need to know, in order for them to be better informed, than expressing speculations upon next weeks 'soap' episode! or supporting a particular political philosophy. The fact is that we are being caught up in an excessive struggle by a few sections of the media in 'competing sensationalism', sometimes to virtual hysterical levels. It might improve 'circulation' results, but this is NOT good for DEMOCRACY! And it DOES affect Ofcom's regulation concerning 'distortion of facts'. As already mentioned, the problem is that this pursuit of 'sensationalism' tends to hide vitally important information that the people should be told about. In this regard I decided to record the front-page headlines of all the morning newspapers. To do this I decided, entirely by random choice, a future date when I would list all the headlines in the morning newspapers. I will not quote which date this was, so as to avoid being accused of causing selective unfair criticism. On the day selected I found the following front-page headlines for eight of that day's morning newspapers.

- Four newspapers, giving detailed criticism of a business 'tycoon'.
- A 'blackmail' scandal against a nation's leader.
- Alleged clues concerning a missing child.
- The tax affairs of a former, very popular, UK comedian.
- 'Chaos' at the horse races caused by horse flu!

How many of these front-page headlines help to make the people better informed of vitally important 'news' (like 'inconvenient truths' see paragraph below). Can it not be argued from a 'moral responsibility' point of view (more of this subject later), that more attention should be devoted to – say – the country's true situation for business, health, education, crime and so on. Then the people would be better informed and thus be more able to give a better qualified consistent view of the true state of the nation and its government, particularly when elections and referendums are to be held.

Within this book alone, as an ordinary citizen, after careful research, I have located many hidden and serious truths about some very serious situations (the UK's national debt, hidden reductions in public services, serious regional inequality etc.) which never hit the front pages. Should we not question the national press and the media why some of these facts, unearthed by responsible, professional independent sources, given in this book, were not given the same front-page publicity they thoroughly deserve, rather than the kind of headlines, on one day, quoted above?

However, on the other hand, and to the credit of the UK's national daily morning newspapers, on a certain date in November 2021, the following front-page headlines appeared on five newspapers.

- 'Government person' has made at least £X.M from second job.
- 'Government person' in peril over 'moonlighting'.

- £5 million 'government person' with no shame.
- 'Government person', house of greed.
- 'Government person' admits misleading a court.

When the media can suddenly all 'come out of the closet' with important facts for the people, like these above, restoring true democracy still remains a possibility, but still protects the aspect of 'media freedom'.

Again, during my 'ramblings' around news programmes on the TV, and the press media, about Brexit. I became increasingly aware of the uniformity of a large section of the media in claiming that Brexit will be a complete disaster. I found one exception to this in April 2019 concerning the decision at that time to delay the day for the UK's exit from the EU. Without naming the newspaper concerned I quote an opinion (matrix) which said 'Yesterday was a truly dark day for British democracy. This extension (date of leaving the EU) means we will remain trapped under the rule of an undemocratic bureaucracy which has little interest in the UK's future. The long-term effect of this will poison our democracy for decade to come'. When you also consider that all three main political parties then had policies against Brexit, and that a number of multinational companies and the banks tend to oppose Brexit, despite the referendum result from the people, I became a bit more suspicious. Then, one day, through my letter box came a leaflet extolling the virtues of a particular chain of pubs, hotels and restaurants. (I will not give the name for fear of being accused of 'advertising'.) The leaflet included a statement from the organisation's chairman which I, personally, was delighted to read! I quote. 'The public, PM, businesses and the media have been the subject of a cunning plan by the elite metropolitan voices – which lost the (UK) EU referendum. The cunning plan... is that leaving the EU without a deal is a cliff edge, a leap in the dark and a walk into a fiery inferno'. The statement went on with 'This cliff edge talk is nonsense. Everything you (the customer) buy from the EU can be brought from within the United Kingdom or the 95% of the world outside the EU'. My perspective is that this is not a case of 'the exception that proves the rule' it is 'the exception which proves a considerable level of non-transparency'. All credit to those who provided us with the contrary view.

One of the many people I admire in today's world is the former vice president of the USA, Al Gore, who gave the world three words of enormous significance, 'An Inconvenient Truth'. He was, as many of us now know, giving the first substantial warning to the whole world of the growing problem of global warming, caused by mankind, in relation to pollution of the oceans, air pollution, deforestation and so on. Now, thankfully, this is known throughout the world, and both environmentalists and the people are able to start making demands for change. And, to their credit, the media has now added their voice to help deal with this problem. But here we have a case where, yet again, people throughout the world were being kept in the dark about an exceptionally serious global problem. We need more Al Gores to uncover other 'inconvenient truths' that the world's leaders are hiding from us, the people.

Having said all this, I must again acknowledge that the UK's media, with one or two rare exceptions, is consistently of a high standard and is respected throughout the free world. It would have been virtually impossible to research a subject of this book's title without careful reference to the UK media reports. To illustrate this point, let me quote just three examples (from a very long list) of cases reported during January 2019, where freedom of the press is seriously threatened, and basic standards are ignored solely for political power and self-interests in other part of the world. And these incidents continue to happen today

- (January 2019) 'Vietnam has begun the new year by clamping down on internet freedom with a new law that makes criticising the communist government online a criminal offence'.
- (January 2019) 'Netflix has been criticised for removing an episode of a satirical comedy series in Saudi Arabia because it was deemed to be too critical of the kingdom's rulers. The episode criticised a Saudi crown prince over the (outrageous)

murder of a Saudi journalist who was a vocal critic of the kingdom's rulers.'

- (January 2019) 'Russian MPs back a new move to outlaw "Fake news". Gaol sentences to be given to anyone who "insults" the state' (i.e., the ruling 'elite').

There are countless examples of zero press freedom throughout the whole world. This situation, combined with many other factors (dictator-ism, wars, fraud, discrimination etc. etc.) fully justifies two words in this book's title, i.e., 'catastrophic crisis') So far as the UK is concerned, with a few carefully worded improvements we would set an important updated yardstick for the world to follow.

One piece of advice, which I was given by an academic tutor many years ago, I would like to pass on in connection with reading newspapers and watching the news media on TV. It was this. 'Try to identify, over a reasonable period of time, which newspaper headlines support, or oppose, the actions of the UK's "government of the day". Quite often, it will become quite clear, particularly from the front-page headlines, who they support. Then you can form your own conclusions upon how some parts of the national media are, by stealth, trying to influence your opinions and beliefs.'

Our opinions and beliefs ARE influenced by whatever sources of information we choose to read, hear, see and note, and the media, the press and TV does have a major influence on our opinions, viewpoints and prejudices. The media and press can be very political without making it too obvious. I will only suggest that, acknowledging the essential need for press freedom, we vary our press reading habits, look at other TV news channels, and if a particular matter concerns or worries you, take the time to do a search on the web for independent, non-political facts. Your votes at all elections are vitally important. It is one of the most important ways to bring about change and reduce the power of an elite few who put their own interests before those of the nation and its people. Your single vote does count. Take the advice to seek the truth from varying sources on area's which are important to you and our nation. Don't be a 'lemming' and go with the crowd. You have a right to hold your own views. Do please, however, seek actual verifiable facts beforehand. Please, please go to the trouble of voting at every election afterwards. The increasing rate of non-voters (see later chapter) is a serious danger to our democracy level.

What is my own perspective on this aspect of democracy? I believe the media itself needs to update their own standards to provide media news services which are verifiable, truthful, balanced, fair and undiscriminating on matters which readers need to be aware of. Then they can form less influenced views upon the nation's problems. 'Trust the collective wisdom of the people' is a guideline that responsible politicians should apply upon matters of national importance. So far as the media is concerned, as it is the people who pay for newspapers and the media, they have a right to expect truthful reports (not propaganda) to improve their collective wisdom, as well as sports features, advertisements and editorials.

There is yet another abuse of the news media on the web. You can test this out for yourself. Go onto one of the many 'news' pages, pick out the headlines that attract your interests and open up the headline article. You will begin to see that the 'headlines' are all carefully selected and controversial intended ONLY to encourage as many people as possible to open the article. What do you get? Two or three sentences relative to the headline, followed by endless advertisements, before asking you to continue to the 'next page', which you do and this is followed by more and more advertisements. 'Web news'? It is just one big trick to use controversial headline subjects to hide pressurised advertising, with nothing to do with the original advertising.

At the time of reviewing this chapter (March 2022), the media was 'sensationalising' the 'Partygate' scandal, where, as my readers will recall, a party was held at 10 Downing Street, attended by the prime minister, during the coronavirus pandemic, contrary to the law against social gatherings (created by the current government in power). He and others were found 'guilty' of this offence. (One rule for one... etc.). Whilst I have voiced my opposition to both extreme capitalism and extreme socialism, and the inequality sometimes of the UK's legal system, so far as 'classes' of population are concerned, for the sake of fairness, I thought the 'sensationalising' of this incident was somewhat unfair. How many, I ask, of all 'levels' of our nation did the same thing, at the same time, and were never brought to justice. Of course, I expect, no 'media' parties were held at the same time, were there?! ('Let he that is without guilt, caste the first stone.')

Finally, on a slightly 'lighter' note upon news reporting, do I recall correctly reading in one national daily newspaper (no names or dates!) a headline 'MP asks for stronger gin in the House of Commons'. Double or triple strength gin should be provided in the 'Commons', an MP has suggested. (To quote) 'In these troubled times ... we could all do with a bit of extra'. A small sign of humanity, perhaps? Or just blatant alcoholism! At least he did say 'all'!

Social Responsibility

'Social responsibility' was a term I came across some years ago, but it seemed to me at the time, not to be significant. But it cropped up again during my research for this book, so it appeared to be worth a second, more thorough study. Again, I found that my original reaction was entirely wrong. 'Social responsibility' is a subject that identifies important circumstances in the search for a higher standard of democracy.

So, again, let us identify what the current day interpretation of 'social responsibility' is and then address the question as to its relationship to democracy. 'Wikipedia' (website encyclopaedia) provides us with the following. 'Social responsibility is an ethical framework and suggests that an entity, be it an organisation or an individual, has an obligation to act for the benefit of society at large. It is a duty every individual must perform so as to maintain a balance between the economy and the ecosystems'. This definition goes on with 'social responsibility means sustaining equilibrium between the two. It pertains not only to business (and government), but also to everyone whose actions impacts on the environment'. (To which I would emphasise 'all aspects of the environment including, specifically, 'people').

Other definitions of social responsibly include such ideals as 'openness and honesty', 'concern of others', 'acceptance of responsibility for actions', 'justice', 'equality' and 'privacy'. The principals of both 'commercial social responsibility' and 'civic social responsibility' strongly support the principles of true democracy because of the duty towards society, as a whole. Of serious concern to my mind is applying relevant, specific values that benefit society, rather than the needs of an 'elitist' group or any specific geographical area.

The problem is that social responsibility is neither a requirement, duty, nor obligation enforceable by legal statute. There are no yardsticks to measure the extent – or absence – of such things as 'openness and honesty'; 'acting for the benefit of society at large'; 'acceptance of responsibility for actions taken' and so on. My view, because of the vital importance of social responsibility aspects, is that there must be measurable and testable standards laid down which relates to the criterion of social responsibility. Where these standards are not met, the offending individual or organisation should be publicly identified; this would be followed with an effective financial punishment on a scale relative to the damage caused to society as a whole. Such measures and others suggested would also provide more facts to the people enabling them to form more accurate views at times of elections, and choices of products and services. So, is this not the time where individual, social, business and civic responsibility needs to have statutorily supported rules to support and protect our society and environment both collectively and individually? And, because there is growing distrust in the current electoral system, a separate non-political, national people's jury (chosen by lot) should, in my view, be appointed to draft a 'law of social responsibility' in respect of governmental and commercial activities. This 'people's jury' would be supported and advised by independent senior lawyers, the police force, academics from related disciplines and respected independent specialist from commerce. At the time of editing this section/subject (April 2023), I read in the press that 'A move in the USA against the government's foreign policy entitled "people before profit", supports many of the principals of social responsibility'. A small sign of hope for the future perhaps? Time will show.

There is a slightly different type of 'social responsibility'. This is 'ethical responsibility' which argues that in business, ethical responsibility is concerned with actions that affect the world around us. Specifically, this means the following principals:

- Businesses have a responsibility to behave in ways that do not cause unjustified harm, suffering, waste or destruction.

- Ethical responsibility enables us to understand who, or what, a company's actions, affect.

The problem, again, is that the commercial world presumes that the pursuit of profit outweighs any other consideration. 'Ethical responsibility' therefore runs contrary to this all-embracing aim. My perspective is that provided it can be fully proved that any product which clearly causes harm on a national scale should result in the commercial organisation concerned being heavily fined, by being charged with a new 'environment tax'.

The above principals of social responsibility as defined above CAN become legally enforceable. The protests of those who would be against these concepts would only come from people with vested personal interests and for once, such protests need to be fairly evaluated and if found to be unjustified, rejected outright.

The most critical point in the interpretation of 'social responsibility' are the words 'An organisation has an obligation to act for the benefit of society, as a whole.' In an article in a UK newspaper (January 2020), the heading read '£14 Bn. boost for the arms trade'. To quote the report 'The world's largest arms manufacturers have seen their (market) value raise by nearly £14 Bn in the wake of the assassination of Qassein Soleimani (a Middle East 'leader') As the current confrontation between the USA and Iran continue, funds are expected to increase through lucrative new defensive equipment orders'. Is this not an appalling example that even before any war starts, the commercial 'elite' are making so much money just out of the fear of another war. Do not the people of any nation have any rights to tell their so-called government representatives that they don't want a another war?

Let us apply another simple test of social responsibility in today's world. We have a very serious and growing problem. Global warming. Symptoms and causes. Pollutants and plastics in our oceans, carbon monoxide in our atmosphere, deforestation and uncontrolled use of our planet's resources (land, sea, air, underground), Various life forms simply dying out. Who does this? Commercial organisations. Who uses the products of these activities? Mankind, who are currently not aware of the consequences? Who profits mostly from these activities? Investors, shareholders, directors and political leaders. All with direct personal interests, or simply, for profitability reason. Do people have any say or influence in decisions relating to these activities? No! What are the consequences of these activities continuing? Responsible and knowledgeable scientists are now using words like 'mass extinction of the planet'. Final question. Is any aspect of social responsibility criteria being applied? I leave this question to you to consider. (In a later chapter, we will consider the relationship of democracy decline, to the global environment 'crisis'.)

Is it not time for the rules of social responsibility to be a new standard for the scientific WORLD to adopt in full? I strongly believe so. BUT has the scientific WORLD 'got the bottle' (i.e., be determined enough) to adopt the principals of lsocial responsibility, IN FULL? Or will they succumb to the demands of various elite classes (political, commercial, religious, etc), and thereby contribute towards the end of this beautiful world of ours?

I am a great believer in robust, extensive and fair commercialism. We live in a world of 'trading'. The pursuit of profit is clearly an essential characteristic (and motivation) of a free society able to keep pace (and exceed perhaps) the rest of the world. There are many good sides of capitalism actions and policies. They include but are not limited to increased employment, scientific development, education, social welfare and many more. However, in all essential activities in a free and fair and democratic society, there must exist fair, justified and reasonable levels of regulation. 'Social responsibility' can specify fair criteria as described above, but it does not have a great deal of legal backing. There are laws relating to fraud, libel, theft, copyrights, to name but a few. But 'unbridled capitalism' (or 'socialism'!) in the commercial world remains a real and serious threat to democracy and the people at large. Not convinced? Then take some time to consider truthful and accurate sources of information and facts upon the other side of capitalism, and then measure these alongside the criteria of 'social responsibility'.

Looking at this aspect from a worldwide commercial point of view, I quote, 'the scientific consensus, that humans are altering the world's climate has now passed 99.9%, according to research, that strengthens the case for immediate global action'. This comes from the 'Cop 26' summit in Glasgow (20/10/21). The report goes on 'the degree of scientific certainty about the impact of greenhouse gases is now like a past survey of nearly 90,000 climate related past studies that burning fossil fuels such as oil, gas, coal, peat and trees is heating the planet and causing more extreme weather. "Sceptical voices" argue that mankind is wholly responsible'. Let us pause, for a moment on this claim, and consider who we mean by 'mankind'. Consider the following questions.

- Did we, the people, decide that mountains of plastic, non-recyclable materials should be used extensively for so many different products? And then dumped in the oceans?
- Did we, the people, decide upon the unrestrained use of various types of carbon emitting materials, clouding the atmosphere?
- Did we, the people, approve massive areas for deforestation?
- Did we, the people, allow uncontrolled pollution of our rivers, streams, seas and oceans?

I say NO! to all these. The decisions were based entirely on commercial profit, and government mismanagement, with us the people being kept ignorant of the true consequences. Yes, we have used the materials quoted above, because we had little choice or knowledge of the consequences. Sorry, blaming 'mankind' is neither accurate or justified. Who allowed the four examples listed above to occur? Governments and the commercial world 'elite', NOT the people!

So let's, for the moment, allow ourselves a bit of 'satire' and imagine how national interests might have been ignored in 'boardrooms' and governmental committees. Consider the following imaginary scenarios.

- (Boardroom scene). 'What is this plastics thing that the technical director keeps banging on about?' Answer. 'It's a far cheaper material and can be produced as a very wide use container material, sold worldwide'. Response. 'OK, get on with it, but we want to see big profits, or you are out of a job!'
- (Boardroom scene). 'Have you seen this report upon a possible better treatment for pregnant women?' Response. 'Yes, it's a much cheaper version of treatment for depression and can be mass produced for a wide market. There does not seem to be any side effects at all.' Response. 'OK, get on with it'.
- (Government discussion behind closed doors). 'We got a very large and helpful contribution for our

election costs, from a (building trades conglomerate), which enabled us to influence the general election result in our favour. What can we do to ensure the same treatment next time?' Answer. 'We could put up an argument for more house building and TELL local planning authorities to be more flexible in allowing more housing development.' Comment. 'This means we will lose much more open space and woodland.' Response. 'So!?'

- (Government discussion behind closed doors). 'We are getting a lot of pressure from local authorities about increased pollution of rivers and streams from trade waste and inefficient domestic sewage treatment facilities They want more government funding support.' Response. 'Sorry cannot afford that. We have other priorities and there's NO votes in sewage anyway!' (Update 2022. Sewage reports in UK's seas!)

Complying with the principals of 'social responsibility'? I do not think so. The real culprits should be identified and (in my view) severely punished by a new ENVIROMENT TAX. One exception to the above examples (two of which are actually factual) should be made absolutely clear, because the 'elite' will try to blame others (e.g., scientists/ technicians). This would be completely unjust. Scientists cannot be expected to know everything. Their research work MUST continue. But with much more research/

effect/investigations upon ALL the possible consequences of innovations without harassment from the 'elite'. It is the decision makers who are at fault.

In a more recent article (December 2021) upon past 'inventions' now known to be disastrous worldwide, were clearly defined. The coal industry, leaded petrol, thalidomide drugs for depressed pregnant women, chlorofluorocarbon (or 'CFC') to 'safely' cool fridges and public spaces, all later known to be resulting in a 'hole' in the planet's ozone layer, are just a few of 'mankind's actions?' past mistakes. I, being one of 'mankind', being responsible? NO WAY!

In the past (and at a 'lower' level), the BBC used to feature a series of programmes of the TV series 'Watchdog'. In my view, another excellent source of 'inconvenient truths'. This programme gave a series of reports, backed up by facts, reports and detailed research of many, many 'bogus' small time commercial activities, which seriously harmed vulnerable, ordinary people and the environment on a more local level. The programme describes a wide variety of commercial and crooked deceptions against people throughout the UK. It clearly demonstrates the opposite of social responsibility, being (in my words), 'Profit (thefts) at ANY price!' How many of these cases ever find their way to courts of law, resulting in fair compensation for the victims, and appropriate punishment for those responsible? I accept that in some cases, notably large corporations, people ARE compensated. All credit to those organisations. However, there are those who are not so lucky, for example these businesses who go out of business only to reopen under a different name. This situation is a minute (very small) example of what should happen worldwide. The point is that if this kind of investigation can be carried out in 'local matters', why not for NATIONAL ISSUES?

Without harming the essential benefits of 'responsible' commercial concerns, we need to have more statutory control which gives the people more protection, assesses reasonable compensation, and, say, in cases of bankruptcy, punishes the offenders. Added to these would be a requirement, worded by independent scientists, specifying HOW considerably more prior research could be carried out, into the long-term consequences of ANY new material, systems activities, new products or materials.

In an article given by 'UNESCO', on the subject of 'science in society', we are told that 'science is the greatest collective endeavour. It contributes to ensuring a longer and healthier life, monitors health, provides medicine to cure diseases, helps to provide water for our basic needs including food, energy and makes life better'. Good words. That is true and how it should be. Sadly, there is another side to scientific endeavour. It is this. The 'elite' pressure science in other areas, superficially to improve their own 'standing' in the minds of people. There is a picture which I once saw in the media which I will never forget which illustrates my fears about science's 'social' responsibilities. (It is said, is it not, 'that a picture is sometimes worth more than a thousand words'?). This picture showed an annual military parade in Moscow, Russia. It showed thousands of soldiers in strict parade order, but with the most gigantic weapons of mass destruction (nuclear missiles), and the picture of the then Russian leader, gloating on the scene, with thousands of Russian people, all with proud smiles on their faces. HOW BLOODY AWFUL! HOW BLOODY DISGRACEFULL! What a wonderful achievement by our beloved leader to keep us 'safe'! How can such weapons developed by scientists, on the orders of the 'elite', satisfy the rule 'science FOR society'? Social responsibility, benefits for all?

Applying some of the principals of 'social responsibility' within our laws would be another good start in improving true democracy (management FOR the people) in both governmental and commercial activities.

Where Democracy is Either Non-existent or 'Undermined'

Again, let us start by defining the circumstances which arise where, in this beautiful world of ours, democracy fails, is rejected outright, or historically has never really been implemented. We can begin to remind ourselves of the answers to the first question of what constitutes 'democracy'. ('Rule by the people for the people', 'equality', 'regular free and fair elections of a nation's government', and so on). And we considered the definition of the opposite of democracy, 'oligarchy' ('rule by an unelected elite', 'secrecy', 'downward government of decisions', and so on). There are, of course many more circumstances which demonstrate the lack of democracy. Historically the names of infamous dictators are easy to recall. Adolf Hitler, Mussolini, General Franco to name just three from Europe alone. And finally, other actions and consequences of 'no democracy'. Wars, terrorism, militarism, religious atrocities, poverty, complete breakdown of law and order, brutal oppression, propaganda rather than transparency, unrestricted capitalism, extreme socialism and so on.

The next question is, what reliable evidence is there to show, where, in this beautiful world of ours, are the nations and areas where democracy does not exist. Additionally, sadly, there are nations which classify themselves as 'democratic', but, by their own actions demonstrate that they are certainly not so. Fortunately, we live in a (not perfect!) democratic nation and region of the world where we have access to 'fairly' truthful news reports and we have regular, usually four-yearly general elections. So, in this respect, I have extracted from one UK newspaper (the 'i'), news items which accurately describes and demonstrates the consequences of the absence of democracy. The following list of news items is taken from a six-month period, between September 2018 to April 2019. (I must repeat yet again, that all UK newspapers are published to a fairly high standard, and I quote from only one such source.) So, here are the extracts of relevant news items I particularly noted. I simply give the date of each report. Do be mindful that situations will have changed since the dates indicated. The reports were fairly accurate at that time. I emphasise this list is the 'tip of the iceberg'. The following quotes should be viewed as an accurate sample of the kind of circumstances which are actually arising today, demonstrating the real existence of 'oligarchy'.

- 27th Sept. 2018 Austria. 'Far right ruling party tries to gag critical news media'. Austria's Internal Ministry has been caught compiling a list of 'critical' media outlets for distribution to the country's police forces with orders to limit the information given to journalists from those organisations.
- 15th Oct. 2018 Russia. An opposition leader of a demonstration objecting to government plans to raise the pension age was imprisoned for 20 days for staging an 'illegal protest'. (Note. See final chapter upon 'Remedies UK'!)
- 8th Nov. 2018 Iran. Iran has been hit by a wave of protests by people during the last year, pointing fingers at the rich and powerful ('elite'), including clerics, diplomats, officials and their families.
- 4th Dec. 2018 Hong Kong, China. 'A pro-democracy Chinese lawmaker has been banned from standing for election because he implicitly supports Hong Kong's independence from China'. (Readers will be aware that this matter has been the result of more recent large demonstrations by Hong Kong people, in support of this concept).
- 5th Dec. 2018 Rohingya. 'Muslins are fleeing from Myanmar and Bangladesh to Malaysia and Indonesia's Sumatra, following a crackdown on "peoples smugglers".'
- Venezuela. 'Refugees are fleeing into neighbouring countries from poverty, violence and imploding social and medical inequalities.'

- Algeria Chadri Bendedid postponed the second round of the nation's parliamentary elections in 1991 because he was worried the Islamist groups might win. He was then forced to resign, and civil war was the result. (My comment. A good example of 'political guile' and unrestrained religious fanaticism, so creating a war.)
- Egypt. 'Hosni Mubarak deferred Egypt's 2006 local government vote because he feared the result would threaten a parliamentary poll.'
- Jordan. King Abdullah deferred a general election in 2001 for two years because of 'political tensions'.
- United Kingdom. Whilst we in the UK enjoy a small level of democracy (as this book claims), it is very much 'not perfect'. For the sake of 'fairness' therefore, it seems to me to be right that a note of criticism should be included in this list of the UK So here is one example of our failings. Before the UK Brexit referendum, all the three main political parties (Conservative, Labour and Liberal) made a solemn public promise to abide by the result of the people's vote. (The most likely reason being that they all expected the result to be against Brexit.) After the result of the vote showed that a small yet significant majority was for Brexit, all three parties changed their minds and many. MPs began a campaign to block Brexit. This went on for three years following the referendum result. Sadly, this is

yet another example of many on this list, where it is a common political tactic of nation's leaders and government members to delay applying the specified wishes of the people when they do not want to, in the hope that different circumstances arise (or are 'created'), which justifies not implementing the wishes of the electorate. (This question has now been resolved following the 2019 general election where the voters once again expressed the same view in favour of Brexit.) The political party's leader who gave a public promise to carry out the people's wishes (where, to his credit, he has been true to his word) was elected back to power.

Secondly, why is your own vote so important? You will see that answer to that question given on the list of election results since 1945, and the last four results. How can we have a government in power when so many either voted AGAINST the incoming government AND A LARGE PROPORTION FAILED TO EVEN VOTE! Is this 'democracy'? Is this 'governmental representativeness'?

- 18th January 2019 China. 'Assault on human rights at the worst level since 1989 (being the Tienanmen Square massacre of demonstrators), in China.' A report by the Human Rights Watch, in its annual report, names China amongst its top concerns. Human rights defenders in China are subject to arbitrary detention, imprisonment and enforced 'disappearance', according to this report. (Recall entry for 4th December 2018 above.)

- 1st Feb. 2019 A blank envelope was included in this newspaper edition, unadressed, but with a statement on the envelope which said, 'A lot of people want you to throw away this envelope'. Clearly, I did not. It turned out to be a letter from 'Amnesty' inviting subscriptions and support for their work in human rights worldwide. The letter records the kind of things that happen in the worst cases of inhumanity where democracy is non-existent. To quote just three example cases only.

  The general in Myanmar who ordered the ethnic cleansing of Rahimyar people by murder, rape and burning their homes.

  A military commander in the 'Democratic (!) Republic of Congo' who ordered his men to rape women and girls as a tactic to humiliate the 'enemy'.

  A dictator in North Korea that sends thousands of citizens to suffer and die in slave labour camps.

  (Comment. A respected worldwide organisation like Amnesty International would simply NOT make claims of this sort that were not completely true).

- 28th Feb. 2019 India/Pakistan. 'Call for calm after clashes raise risk of war between India and

Pakistan'. In 1947, the UK Government granted independence from the then 'UK world empire', to the whole Indian sub-continent with divisions as two separate nations, being India (mainly Hindu) and Pakistan (mainly Muslin). The main reason being to create a more peaceful situation between the two-opposing doctrines. Sadly, another war broke out in 1965 between the two countries and it seemed at that time of this report, a new one was brewing.

Own comment. True democracy and dictatorial religions are NOT compatible. It is yet again, another 'power game'. There must be much more mutual respect between different religious cultures in the whole world, with an uncontested standard of allowing people to engage in peaceful religious beliefs, of their own choosing AND to have full involvement in essential democratic rights and standards. History is littered with hundreds of examples of religious wars, worldwide.

- 29th March 2019 Algeria. ('Hundreds of thousands march for the country's president's removal from office'). An army general has called for the position 'to be made vacant' (which I suspect is the first move to replace one dictator for another). The president announced he would stand for election for yet another term of office to prolong his 20-year rule but agreed he would not stand for election after that. Protesters claim this is a cynical move simply to prolong his rule. They believe that the president's health has declined to such an extent that he is NOT, in fact, ruling at all. They claim that his rule is being carried out by a small, privileged group locally described as 'Le Pouvoir' (the power), comprising of business/family (selected) politicians and military leaders, who are ruling by wholly corrupt and oppressive activities, only concerned with preserving themselves in power/prosperity.

12th April 2019 Sudan. 'Sudan's military coup as hated president is ousted after 30 years in power'. Sudan's military have removed president Omar Bashir, in response to escalating popular people's protests. The defence ministry announced military rule for two years imposing an emergency clampdown that risks inflaming protesters who had demanded civilian democratic change, not another form of dictatorship.

Not worried about all this? Please, you should be. It is my aim, and that of an increasing number of others, to make you worried enough to *do* something. Just combine three worldwide known problems at present. Declining democracy in both the 'developed world' AND the dictatorship-led countries. The most awful weapons of mass destruction (nuclear, chemical, biological etc. now available) *that we know about.* And finally, the growing effects of global warming.

You will note from the dates of the above reports that they are taken from reports during a specified period. This is completely true. But the point is that these situations are a permanent feature in today's world. Whilst researching the respected media for information upon a different aspect of today's democracy later (December 2021) I came across yet another (blatant) example of the 'war' against democracy by a nation's 'elite'. As readers will know, Hong Kong was 'taken over' by China some years ago (much, in my view, to the shame of the UK's government, in power at the time). I now read those conditions for true democracy are being literally banned by the Chinese socialist dictatorship, in relation to governmental elections in Hong Kong. Firstly, the proportion of parliamentary seats were reduced for Hong Kong and 'only candidates' who passed a test of loyalty to the 'Beijing elite' were allowed to stand. 'Activists' in Hong Kong were arrested for urging their fellow citizens NOT to vote. (At the previous election only some 25% of the people actually voted). Yet another example that BOTH extreme socialism and capitalism are totally against democracy. (The article in question, to their credit, goes on to suggest justified actions by the UK to combat this growing worldwide problem. Too right!) In my view we (UK) should never have abandoned the Hong Kong people to the mercies of the Chinese dictatorship in the first place without, at least, calling a referendum of the Hong Kong people.

In a more recent excellent article issued from 'Expresso Communications' (Jan. 2023) on the web, 20 reasons were listed defining 'how capitalism is bad for humanity'. To respect copyright principles I will only list the first five, and strongly recommend my readers to download the full list from their web page. The first five are

1. WILDLIFE is disappearing at an alarming rate.
2. Capitalism upholds PATRIARCHY, a social rule based on holding real power by men.
3. POOR nations. Capitalism breeds competition between countries and perpetuates poverty among developing nations due to individual interests of private corporations.
4. Capitalism perpetuates inconceivable rates of wealth inequality, quoting the income of a founder member of a worldwide supplier of goods and services.
5. Capitalism driven climate change has caused extreme weather events and national disasters during the past few years.

I strongly urge my readers to visit Expresso Communications website and view the remaining 15 reasons and you will see truisms which are being kept from the peoples of the whole world. (For the sake of fairness, my personal view remains as expressed earlier.

Extreme SOCIALISM can also be 'charged' with the same offences against the human race). Our only remedy to fight this disgraceful growing situation is to DEMAND real democracy, where the people make the decisions upon vital matters, having been provided with accurate, relevant and truthful FACTS.

Other well-respected authors and (non-political) researchers have repeatedly warned us of the consequences of the increasing loss of democracy. The above examples represent an exceptionally small sample. It is not even 'the tip of the iceberg'. There are hundreds, perhaps thousands of similar cases throughout the world. In Robert Preston's outstanding book *WTF* he rightly, and very worryingly, describes the 'whole world' areas of tension and instability. Europe, Russia, America, the Middle East, China and the Far East. Terrorism, warlike activities, oppressive religious wars, all have a growing situation clearly and only caused by the power ambitions of various types of political, religious, socialistic, capitalistic dictatorships and national leaders.

Again, in Niheer Dasandi's excellent book *Is Democracy Failing?* he rightly states 'History shows that no system of a nation's government has provided more freedom, prosperity, stability and safety than in a (true) democracy'. He confirms 'One only needs to look at reports of outrageous cruelty, war and famine arising from countries where democracy is either very poor or non-existent, clearly through various forms of dictatorships.' How very, very true!

(Comment). One of the many things we can be proud of in the UK is the continuing warm relationship between our monarchy and most of our people. In one European country, it used to be said 'Parliament rules, but the king reigns'. (Not so today). I, personally, remain a strong advocate for the UK's royalty. The monarch no longer has the power to dictate to the government, but their continued presence, with the monarch's current responsibilities, means there is little room for a dictator! I believe that if the UK's people, given the opportunity to do so, would, overwhelmingly, demand our monarchy remain. Long may this continue! We have shown to the world a clear example of how a former dictatorship situation can be changed in a positive way!

The last example I will quote in this list arises from an article in a well-respected UK Sunday newspaper published in September 2018, which was, for me, deeply shocking. I quote. 'In a secret location in a European city, a locked vault exists monitored by security cameras. It stores 265 identical cardboard brown boxes on metal shelves, looking quite innocuous, but the contents are dreadfully chilling. The boxes contain documents describing top secret intelligence reports detailing Syria's systematic torture and murder of approximately 500,000 people, and 5 million fleeing the country.' This all happened during the rule of Bashar Al Assad in 2011 to 2014. He was never brought to trial. Now (2018), he was on the verge of taking back almost complete control of the country. Which nation put forward Assad in 2011? The UK! The newspaper concerned in this case has a high reputation, worldwide, for revealing the truth in many areas. Did the UK people know about this at the time? Almost certainly NOT.

More recently, in May 2020 (web news, Associated Press), an article was published entitled 'Trump's (US president) emergency powers worry some senators and legal experts'. We read the day he declared the COVID-19 pandemic a 'national emergency', President Trump made a cryptic offhand remark. He said (it is claimed) 'I have the right to do a lot of things that people do not even know about' (!). Apparently (the article states) 'dozens of USA's statutory authorities become "available" to any president where national emergencies are declared. This (true) rule is rarely used, but Trump stunned legal experts and others when he claimed (mistakenly) 'that he had total authority, over state governors in easing COVID-19 guidelines'. As one senator commented, 'Somebody needs to look at these things. This is a case where the president can declare an emergency and then say "because there is an emergency, I can do this and this and this"'. I cannot resist making a comment about this. All politicians say stupid things from time to time ('off the cuff'), and due allowance (and understanding) should be given in this case where the matter is not particularly serious. Nevertheless, this report worries me enormously, on three points. Here we have one of the top world leaders apparently making a claim that he has unlimited (dictatorial) power, whenever he chooses to declare a national emergency. Whatever the true situation is, if his claims are TRUE, democracy is seriously undermined in one of the most powerful nations in the world. If his claim is UNTRUE (because he does NOT have such power) then he does not know what he is bloody well talking about! And thirdly, if the media are misquoting him (for whatever reasons) we should still be worried!

A friend of mine, who holds similar views as myself about the real state of democracy in the UK, asked me how I would react, if I went into a grocery store with a sum of money, and the store's manager told me to give the money to him and he would then decide how the money would be used without any reference to yourself. Also, he would advise you that a proportion of your money, would be used upon other items about which you would be given NO information. My reaction was to tell the manager to 'Gpxx86bb' OFF! And then leave the shop and go elsewhere. (I leave it to you to use your own choice of the first word!) My friend then reminded me that I pay income tax, national insurance contributions, VAT, rates and 'stealth taxes' and have NO say in what the payments are used for. The 'inconvenient truth' is that we have no option but to accept inadequate health services, reduced police services, education, the (REAL unknown) national debt, and many forms of 'austerity' policies.

During the outrageously prolonged negotiations between the UK and the EU over the Brexit matter, it was reported that France would 'block' (veto) any delay to Brexit, unless the UK had a clear objective based on a new choice by the British people. The choice by the British people had already been made in the original referendum. It was simple and clear. The people wanted OUT. The general election which followed firmly confirmed this. The point here is that a leader from one nation was threatening to overrule the wishes of the people in a different nation!

In another article in a reputable UK newspaper (August 2020) the subject of the current UK Government's political propaganda during the coronavirus pandemic, a writer described the government's endless public TV announcements in trying to control the increasing numbers of infected people as 'pointless and clumsy gestures'. The author (no less a person than a high court judge, apparently) commented that 'King Canute' did NOT actually command the incoming sea tides to retreat from his throne on the sandy shore'. But the current UK Government is having a very good go at it! (How very apt in today's world.)

In another case involving Brexit, in March 2019 a web news item claimed that the UK Government had 'taken back some of the powers' in future Brexit policy. This was being done by giving MPs a 'free vote' (individual choice for once), indicating their own preferences upon various alternative government actions following the first referendum result. Nine different choices were offered to the MPs, some of which was to REVERSE the result of the people's referendum, where the people voted OUT. It was assumed that the government (in practice meaning the 'cabinet') were not obliged to accept the referendum result. One or two daily newspapers applauded this as 'taking back control'! Rule by the people for the people? NO. Abuse of power. This free vote failed, and the people said so at the next general election. I recall another saying I once read (I do not recall from where) that 'True power in the UK is achieved by political leverage, rather than the wishes of the people'!

A 2018 'MORI' survey relating to the level of trust and confidence which people have in various elements of society, found that over 90% of those surveyed would trust doctors and medical staff, but less than 20% would trust politicians. Only one third believed MPs would work in the national interest and the same proportion believed MPs would actually represent the people's interests, when contacted by their constituents upon various matters.

Again, in Niheer Dasandi's excellent book *Is Democracy Failing?* he rightly states 'History shows that no system of a nation's government has provided more freedom, prosperity, stability and safety than in a (true) democracy'. How very, very true! Niheer goes on to describe what one 'national president' (I wonder who!) has done so far. Amongst his detailed list are:

- Damaged the nation's democratic institutions.
- Targeted the nation's independent judiciary with public criticisms.
- Appointed family members to government positions.
- Furthered his own personal wealth substantially.
- Sacked key government officials for purely personal reasons.
- Associated with dictators from other nations.
- Circulated 'fake news' to increase his personal support.
- Criticised the media publicly, almost daily.

I think, these being true, this is a clear example of 'oligarchy', the opposite of 'democracy' Which nation do you think was being referred to? Middle East dictatorships? Extreme Communism? Military dictatorships? Religious dictatorships? NO to all of these. The nation's leader begins with 'T' (second name) ruling a major 'democratic nation'.

One of the consequences of the worldwide decline in democracy, which must be noted, I fear, is upon nations where democracy still prevails. It relates to the millions of refugees fleeing from their own totally non-democratic, dictatorship-led nation, seeking refuge in 'better' and more democratic countries. In the case, of just our own UK nation, an article in a respected daily newspaper (December 2021) reports '1,000 people intercepted whilst crossing the English Channel in (just) four days'. This article (at THAT time) states 'more than 27,000 people have reached the UK from France, since the start of the year'. From this fact alone, is it not unreasonable to presume that the actual figure could be much higher still? (We are now seeing the consequences of Russian troops invading the Ukraine.) The UK population is thus growing out of all control, but the geographical size of our island is not! More people, more housing, more roads, more schools, more shops, more factories and offices is clearly one guaranteed result. Another is a most serious environmental impact through loss of open spaces, countryside, woods and forests, greater pollution on land sea and air, when land area is not growing. It must be said. Other nations in Europe have far more space than the UK. Impact on our own democracy? We have yet to see! The remedy, which I will keep repeating, is to deal with the root cause of the problem, in the refugees' own nation, not just the symptoms of the problem. Final updating of this section of the book (April 2023), I read in the national press that Italy is declaring a state of emergency, as migrant numbers surge.

Finally, perhaps by far, the worst example of the absence of democracy can be summed up in one simple word: WARS. Have a look at the following ten questions, and my own perspective answers, and then consider your own.

Question: Of all the billions of different kinds of 'living things' on this planet of ours, which one fights the most 'wars' amongst its own? (The human race.)

Question: Have Human beings got an extensive and worldwide history of war? (Yes.)

Question: Who fights and pays (in terms of costs/deaths) for wars? (Ordinary people.)

Question: Do ordinary people ever get the chance to support or oppose wars? (No.)

Question: Who then, decides upon war decisions? (People's leaders.)

Question: Do leaders ever go to war themselves nowadays? (No.)

Question: Who specifically makes, or influences war decisions? (Dictators, political/religious leaders, etc.)

Question: What is the cost of war in terms of resources and deaths? (So high, it is impossible to give a cost.)

Question: What benefits are obtained from wars? (Advancement of 'war' sciences. Considerable 'profits' for the 'elite'.)

Question: Are there any internationally accepted rules to control war activities? (No.)

I hope these ten questions highlight more 'inconvenient truths' and that my own short answers may be, tolerably, somewhere near the truth. However, to be fair, if one nation starts to invade or seriously threaten another nation (to do so), without reasonable justification, the rights of self-defence must be acknowledged. I have no issue with this concept. Civil wars (internal wars) raise the same principle, but they have a nasty habit of overflowing onto other countries often because of 'defensive pacts', commercial greed, and, of course, the pursuit of personal power.

The pursuit and extension of personal power by the few (political/business national leaders) over the many, in order to vastly increase their power, authority AND personal prosperity, with the consequential decrease in the quality of lifestyles of the people, AND during wars (created by the few), the awful level of fatalities, injuries, etc., etc., is an absolute worldwide disgrace!

Wars have to be prevented, unless there is a genuine, verifiable justification of self-defence. And this means a nation must have the resources (only) to defend themselves. To my knowledge, as a citizen, the only recent worldwide criteria to control/prevent war was summed up by the 'MAD' principal ('Mutually Assured Destruction'), which came into being since the development of weapons of mass destruction (WMDs). This principal needs to be vastly extended by a worldwide protocol, clearly specifying where wars ARE justified and when they are NOT, and thereafter, naming the true causes and culprits where such a protocol is abused. Again, this work can, at present, only fall onto the only 'world authority' we have at present, the United Nations. They need to be empowered by most of the world's nations to the forming of a judiciary authority for investigating wars between nations after clearly specifying the new worldwide protocol.

Banned from membership of such a body would be world leaders (And their supporters) and dictators (political, military, religious etc.). Membership would be limited to a combination of worldwide professionals in relevant disciplines, who are completely independent, AND worldwide ordinary citizens, chosen by 'lot' (e.g., 'Numbers out of a hat'), who can meet predetermined conditions. Such a body would be empowered to investigate threatened or actual war scenarios and to pronounce an open judgement upon whether, or not, a war is justified, and to NAME and shame culprits and causes. Non-involved nations would then be expected to do all they can to stop the war, at least by a complete ban on weapons and other specified forms of support, e.g., commercial OR in the worst-case scenario, independent nations becoming a full supportive ally to the nation invaded.

Because of the availability of these terrible weapons of mass destruction, it enables me to express considerable pride in an historical action by a past UK Government prime minister. None other than our famous Mr Winston Churchill. When Germany invaded Poland in 1939, at the behest of their leader Adolf Hitler, Winston demanded an assurance that Germany would pull out all its armed forces from Poland by a specific date, or the UK would declare war against Germany. They did not. Prime minister then declared 'No such assurance having been received; this country IS at war with Germany'. Despite the most awful consequences on the UK (bombings, thousands of deaths and injuries, etc. etc.) the UK fought the war until its end in 1945. One of the many historical actions for national pride.

So, this is my own list of situations which help justify the book's title and the world crisis. Mankind has now advanced to the point where we DO have the resources, knowledge, technology and systems to stop and reverse democracy decline. Leaders (the 'elite') do not want this. THEN –

The people and their governments must enforce it.

The Abuse of Power

One of the reasons which originally motivated me to try to write this book was that I had seen, in my working years with a local authority, a small number of elected 'representatives' of the people and senior executives were using their positions, clearly, for a variety of 'personal' interests. In a nutshell, they seemed to me to be serving their own interests BEFORE those of the electorate. One such incident I will quote shortly. ('The names and identity of the authority is kept secret to protect the innocent'!) In my innocence I believed (surely) this would never happen in the highest levels of government. My subsequent research of books written by well-respected and knowledgeable authors, and academics, showed, again, how naïve I was. All these sources of information were fully backed up by verifiable facts, which they would hardly publish if they could be shown to be totally false. (My next question was, if the media so loves sensationalism, why do we not read these astounding truisms in the newspapers?) So, I extended my research work onto the web and the more responsible sections of the media press, and books written by very knowledgeable writers. My final perspective? The abuse of power, the higher up you go in all sections of society, whether capitalist or socialistic, is rife! and increasingly/extensively detrimental to democracy and the needs and wishes of people.

I will not, however, burden my readers by page and page of quotations and references from my research areas. Sufficient, I think, to pick out a sample, admittedly my own choice, of simply 12 examples from authoritative sources which seem to me to be the most serious, yet accurate examples, demonstrating the blatant abuse of power. These are as follows.

(Quote). 'In most democracies, big businesses and lobby groups representing powerful economic interests, exert a huge influence on politics, often to the detriment of the majority of citizens' (author Niheer Dasandi, *Is Democracy Failing*). My comment on this most worrying statement is that it is a fundamental requirement in the rules for a genuine democracy for anyone to be able to stand for election to the governing body. This essential requirement is there to ensure the government is made up of people who know and can represent the people's needs and wishes. The reality however, is that for the main political parties to succeed in getting elected involves spending huge sums of supporting finance in publicity and publications, electioneering costs, events, consultancy fees etc. to stand any chance of winning an election. Where does this enormous support come from? The 'elite' extremely rich classes, of course! Do we really believe that the 'nature' of government policies will be to meet the wishes of the people, or those that 'pay the piper'? In the UK Government in 2014, more than half of government ministers attended elite, fee paying schools and half attended Oxford or Cambridge Universities. Given that most of this 'elite' have never experienced the problems that most 'ordinary' people face, how can they truly represent the people's interests? (Again, author Niheer Dasandi.)

- Workers' rights have been severely limited and reduced (discreetly) to gain, control and limit their rights to act against oppressive injustices applied by employers. The old expression was defined as 'downing tools', simply meaning stopping work and going on strike against such things as reducing real incomes/earnings through pay rises well below inflation rates, unjust levels of redundancies and sackings, and expecting more output from workers etc. These rights have been severely controlled by the government, laying down strict new laws and rules which must be met before strike action was classed as 'lawful'. Effectively, workers cannot now afford the personal risks to their livelihoods of 'downing tools' and meeting the new conditions laid down before a strike becomes 'lawful'. The media at the time sensationalised these changes by arguing that past strikes had been wholly influenced by 'left-wing' leaders of the trade unions. NO, THEY WERE NOT! I am old enough to remember that strike actions took place because the work force knew they were being exploited and VOTED, by a large majority, to strike in a free and fair election. How many 'strikes' happen nowadays? Nobody wants to strike unless they are being clearly 'exploited'. Again, what else did the media 'sensationalise'? As many dreadful 'consequences' upon people's lives as they could find of the strike, upon society, all of which was vastly exaggerated. Yet again, more recently, we see clear evidence that our so-called 'representatives of the people', in both the UK's (Conservative/Labour) parties are opposing strike action in two ways. Labour banning its members from joining 'picket lines' of striking workers, and Conservative government laying down even greater controls limiting strike actions (August 2022).

- Coercive control in *religious environments* remains as an extreme example of abusive power over millions of ordinary people. There are so many examples of this. The 'Twin Towers, New York' dreadful calamity strikes, are just one example of many awful actions by human beings against other human beings. 'Go and take over control of three commercial airliners full of innocent people, commit suicide yourself and crash the planes into buildings to kill and injure thousands of innocent people, and you WILL be rewarded by opulence, in heaven'. (It may also increase power and influence for religious leaders!) To be fair, all the religions of the world (including Christianity) have been guilty of similar actions in the past. Once again it is simply, a 'power game' and an abuse of it. It was wholly intended to extend the power and influence of one religion over others. Was this dreadful action in New York decided in accordance with democratic requirements? Of course not! We will perhaps never know the cowards who planned and approved it. The definition of 'oligarchy' was however fully complied with. Of that, there is no doubt. Once again, however, to be fair, we must not forget the other side of religions. The side that cares for others, and gives enormous help and support that is, every day, given freely to support oppressed peoples throughout the world. For this, all credit to them must be firmly recorded and recognised.

- In a later chapter, we will consider the culprits, causes and victims of austerity situations. A worldwide global financial crisis in 2010/11 resulted in many countries applying severe 'austerity' measures to deal with national debts. Did ordinary people cause this situation? No way! Who then caused it? In my perspective, the self-greedy elite classes taking extraordinary risks to acquire personal wealth, risks which did not materialise simply through bad judgement. Who suffered most? Us, the people of course. Greed and stupidity and the abuse of power and influence by the elite was the true cause.

- 'Wikipedia'. In a paper entitled 'Abuse of power and control' very commendably defined many aspects and truisms upon the abuse of power. As with all other sources of information, please just go on the web and read this paper. It is a well-balanced article which defines abusive power, but also gives examples of one or two attempts to control this evil. Most important, in my view, it defines FORMS of institutional abuse and top of the list is 'signs of institutional abuse'. Read it please and you will better understand this most serious problem.

- Whilst working as a 'principal officer' with a local authority quite some years ago, the 'leader of the council' (of the majority political power in power at that time) called a local press conference to give a statement upon how THEY (the political group in power, rather than us the 'workers!') had saved a large amount of public funds so that 'they were now able to allocate more financial resources to 'needy' areas where ever they were needed' (hint, hint, without political prejudices). 'Are we not good?' After answering a few questions from the press representatives, they were thanked for their attendance, and they left the meeting. A colleague of mine was then asked to provide the leader with a copy of the last election results for the authority's area. After a short period of time, the political group then handed out to officers where the funds were to be spent. My colleague and I compared the allocations to the past election results. The areas that got the most allocations were either those where the political groups candidate only just got elected by a narrow majority and those areas where the political groups candidate just missed getting elected. My perspective? A blatant example of using public (OUR) money to buy more power for the local party at the next election. Think this might happen locally sometimes, but not nationally? July/August 2019, a 'Facebook' ad (paid for by cash by the conservatives) heralded a BBC News story reporting that £14Bn cash boost was becoming available for schools, nationally. This ad was removed shortly after it was disclosed that the true figure was £7Bn. Source? Yet another wonderful publication, on this very subject, this time is by Peter Geoghegan entitled *Democracy For Sale.*

Is it not time to DEMAND independently annual audited statements, with nothing left out, of all national funds, which is freely available on the web, as is done in all the lower levels of government? We are talking about how OUR money is being spent!

- Now, we see another example of 'buying votes'. Date 2022. The UK is again in an 'austerity' situation. Again, there are many circumstances for this, but one reason is inescapable. The pursuit of power both internationally and nationally. To which I would add bad management. Trouble is, this has a major impact upon people's voting intentions, when in the UK, a general election is not so far away. 'Oh dear, what can be done about this'!? Up comes a new idea. 'LEVELLING UP POLICIES' of course! So, set up a fund of a few billions which is to be spent in regions of the UK which 'are judged to be' not so well off as other regions. My suspicion is that funds will be used in carefully selected constituencies, where voting intentions supporting the current government have dropped substantially, so that the current local (government) candidate will have a better chance of being re-elected by pointing out the schemes of 'levelling up' improvements. Once again, using OUR public funds to BUY VOTES (back). Perhaps, one day in the future, an independent, non-political, professional association will identify all the areas receiving 'levelling up' funds, and, in some way, evaluate how far this changed voting intentions by the local electorate.

- Going on from the last point, perhaps the most effective weapon which enables abuse and increasing abuse by the 'elite' (as referred to in a previous chapter) is the distorted, untrue, exaggerated propaganda issued and carried out under the full (and increasing) control of global IT conglomerates and, in many cases, paid for from public (OUR) funds (income tax, national insurance, VAT, car parking fees etc., etc.,). Again, in Peter Geoghegan's outstanding book he makes so many verifiable and plausible examples of power abuse by the elite, that I am coming to the belief we, the people, are going to have to be at war with the elite (not of the conventional type of war, but one that 'fights fire with fire') but in a much stronger effective way. In Peter's excellent Chapter 11 ('Democracy going dark') the opening pages refers to a discussion group 'Institute of Government' (a well-respected, highly professional, and independent group) where a point was very well made that 'Britain's electoral laws are fundamentally unfit for purpose where the biggest source of disinformation is the government party, the ones charged with changing the laws of the land'. In yet another book, this time by Jamie Bartlett one of the world's leading experts on the 'digital revolution', he defines how 'IT' is reducing democracy by 'engineering' people's views and prioritising manifesto promises, which can then be dumped, by using carefully selected 'facts', to maintain personal power. Again, these most serious warnings were carefully avoided by the media (not the 'right' sort of 'sensationalism!'). So, to try and put it into simple terms (which 'I' can understand as a typical citizen), it seems to work like this. Firstly, IT conglomerates collectively, in literally millions of ways, extract information every single time you and I use ANY form of IT. This vast amount of information, happening by the microsecond, is no problem for the level of IT available today. Computers then collate the data/information and interprets 'what sells' in the people's mind and what does 'NOT sell'. This is then interpreted into the right 'wordology' that we, ill-informed citizens, like to hear, and so influence our views, and then sell it to whatever 'elite' group is seeking power, mainly governmental or commerce. This creates election-winning manifestos, gets the 'elite' back into more power, after which they are free to do what the hell they like. Commercial elites can take over more of the markets (so reducing choice to the customer and competition). Forget the governments election manifesto, IT will have the best 'worded' answers for doing things or not doing things. The controlled 'sensationalism' in the news items produces wholly unjust, exaggerated, claims upon highly selected subjects, hides important truisms, and again, with the people not realising it, influences their opinions, preferences and choices. Result? The elite become more powerful and the people very much less so. In the final chapter I will refer to the most commendable actions of the UK Suffragettes (votes for women) many years ago. They stood up for their fully justified rights (despite being ridiculed, offended and vilified by the media, again), which they achieved. Winning this vital aspect of democracy was then followed by other nations of the world allowing voting rights for women. All credit to them! As a MAN, I welcome female wisdom and common sense, in the fight to protect true democracy.

- Finally, as a last update upon this subject (April 2023), Amnesty International has circulated a new leaflet upon the subject of people's rights to protest, by us the people, in the United Kingdom. To quote the article's most worrying statement. 'The UK Government wants to shred the Human Rights Act. The law that protects you and I – and our nearest and dearest – from human rights abuses'. This act 'enables us to demand a proper inquiry into the government's handling into (for example) the Covid-19 pandemic'. Well said Amnesty International. Your website should receive more attention from us unwashed, illiterate commoners!

Staying further with this aspect of 'wordology' and IT. There is a 'new?' concept (to me, at least). It is labelled 'expectation management'. At first glance, to me, this seems to be a useful 'tool' in communicating the wishes of people. 'Expectation management' is, I read, 'understanding what people want (or fear) and then making sure they get it OR resolve the problem'. Once that is achieved, popularity, status and reputation is justifiably enhanced. BUT, as with all things there must be conditions and safeguards in order to prevent *exploitation*. For instance, one way might be to use this 'concept' just for the main purpose of increasing personal power. Firstly, when the TRUTH (people wishes and fears) is known, why not admit it BUT with a little bit of exaggeration OR holding back some elements of the truth. This increases public concern, more than is necessary. Then, doing 'more' to 'alleviate' this increased fear (but only to, about the original level!) Personal reputations can thus be enhanced without 'changing' the problem at all. (Any readers of my age warmly, with affection, will recall the radio series 'The Goon Show' and the statement 'FIENDISHLY CUNNING CARRUTHERS, WHAT!?') Remedy? Simple. Let's have ALL the truth, just the TRUTH and nothing less than the TRUTH at the outset!

- This chapter could simply not be complete without reference to possibly one of the world's worst enemies of true democracy. Here is a leader of perhaps the most powerful nation on this planet. Again, quoting from my collection of reference books and reliable information sources, this leader 'regularly accuses media outlets, such as CNN, of spreading "fake news", whilst he, in the same breath, circulates false stories to enhance his support, including threatening political opponents with prison, imposing travel bans on Muslims, exaggerates the size of his supporters, publicly criticises well-respected judges, and appoints family members and favourites to senior positions in government administration'. Thankfully he has now been voted out of office. This from, perhaps, the most powerful nation in the world, claiming to be the most 'democratic'. I need not name the nation concerned, because for one thing, I have enormous respect and admiration of that nation's people, who thoroughly deserve better.

- The declining level of democracy, together with the resulting growing conflicts in the 'middle eastern' region of the world, are now overflowing into more democratic nations in Europe and the American north continent. Terrorist attacks are now an expanding realism, resulting in extreme counter-terrorism measures, which severely affect people's own rights, freedom and safety, so enhancing the power of the various 'elite' classes of the world's other nations.

- As already mentioned, 'PR' is now about influencing public opinion specifically for the single benefit of obtaining, retaining and/or extending power in both the government and commerce elements of society. It is no longer about giving truthful statements of relevance upon matters of public interest. In yet another outstanding book, by Heather Brooke (*The Silent State*) Heather tells us that during the period 1996 and 2008 a London borough doubled its spending on publicity. Another large local authority in the Midlands has spent more than £9m. This is money all paid for by ratepayers and taxpayers in the expectation it is to be used for providing actual public services, education, health, environment etc. Heather's book goes on to quote more historical facts in the increasing levels of central government spending. One example was the 'Central Office of Information' that increased its expenditure by 43% to a whacking £540m in 2008/9. I would 'guess' that the total now must be well over £1Bn. If this kind of money was spent on health, education and the environment, the real-time benefits to the nation's people would be considerable. Whilst Heather's book is now somewhat 'dated' (published in 2010), it is still 'brimming with facts' that fully justify its title. Her 'manifesto for a new democracy' contains nine wholly justified principles, which need US the people to demand full acceptance, in the work to restore real democracy.

- In a most alarming article in the *Independent* in February 2022, headed 'UK edging closer to a "flawed" democracy', reference is given to declining global democracy 'rankings' for the UK, by the organisation 'Economic Intelligence Unit'. The UK has dropped to 18th place behind Taiwan and Uruguay, and just ahead of Mauritius and Costa Rica. Quoted causes were 'party financing', 'series of scandals', 'lack of transparency', and 'ministers and officials failing to follow the rules'. A feeling among people 'that they do not matter and can't change things' was clearly prevalent. A saying that springs to my mind is 'personal power stems from political leverage'. Or put more simply 'you scratch my back and I will scratch yours!' Result? The wrong people get into higher levels of government than they are fit for.

- When we see clear and indisputable evidence of a travesty of justice, priorities, and 'representativeness' by a nation's leader, we, the people EXPECT that the leader's own political party removes such a leader from office. Failure to do so is a serious indictment against the party itself AND its members.

- One other matter concerning rejecting the views and concerns of people (actually throughout the whole world) is the matter of WMDs (Weapons of mass destruction). What are these? They are ballistic missiles containing nuclear, biological, chemical compounds designed to kill thousands of people, towns and cities, on a worldwide scale. The logic behind this is 'if XYZ nation has them we MUST have them as a deterrent'. Do any of my readers remember when these weapons were being developed during the 1950s and 1960s, the mass demonstrations with the 'Ban the Bomb' placards in London and elsewhere? Did it stop the governments of major nations developing these dreadful weapons? No, of course not. These weapons are (again) a way of the 'elite' of the world retaining power! Don't think this? The advice to the people given by the government was along the following lines. 'If you hear a large bang and a flash of light, lay on the ground facing the source and cover your heads with your arms and hands'. (!) This was not the only action taken by the government. Using public funds (provided by us the people) 'Regional seats of government' were constructed. These comprised of below ground, heavily concreted air raid shelters for local MPs, a few 'civil servants' but no one else. Some of these shelters have been dismantled since but some remain, either heavily disguised or built over them. Want to re-activate these people demonstrations today? Sorry, no! The (dreadfully under resourced) police authorities have been given even more rules to limit all such demonstrations. My dream? people from all nations worldwide to demonstrate against their own governments, DEMANDING the banning of ALL WMDs worldwide!

- The final example of the causes of power abuse is not going to be outstandingly popular! But it has to be said. The growing abuse of power is caused – to a large extent – by US THE PEOPLE! We must accept a large part of the responsibility for this most serious and growing problem. In the first case, the growing proportion of 'non-voters' at elections is simply handing over more and more power to the 'elite' classes! 'My vote will not change things' is no better than an excuse not to bother. Can we not realise that the right to free and fair elections is both a right AND a responsibility for all? By not voting, the government elite can interpret this in whatever way they choose, which fits their own ambitions for more power. My plea to all is to vote at every opportunity, and my view, is not to vote for the two major political parties but for ANY of the other parties of your own choice. Recall, in an earlier chapter, I quoted the official government statistics showing that since the end of the Second World War (1945) the UK has been governed by simply one of TWO political parties only. The provable decline in democracy, MUST therefore be on their joint shoulders! If many more people vote carefully, the resulting proportion of votes which both main political parties cannot ignore will send a 'warning shot across their bows' and the commercial 'elite' who funds them. Next, challenge the excesses of certain parts of the press and media, and DEMAND less propaganda. Join a legitimate democracy reform group and support their work. Stop giving your personal details to the millions of commercial data groups (mainly on the web). Attend demonstrations which relate to restoring real power back to you the voters. Demand to have authoritative and verified information upon how YOUR MONEY is being spent. Harass your MP and local councillors with complaints and demands for real public services. Demand genuine re-instatement of workers' rights. Stop accepting the claims and abuses by the media and challenge their actions. Finally DEMAND, again, a new and independently organised referendum upon electoral changes including active participation by the Electoral Reform Society and the Institute of Government.

I will end this chapter by suggesting an additional (minor) addition to the dictionary's interpretations for 'politics'. I suggest an additional new word 'Politicalisation'. Meaning 'to define either good things or bad, in such a way, which attracts "support" from the public/people, for the sole benefit of personal power acquisition and retention'.

SO, IN A NUTSHELL

ONLY US THE PEOPLE CAN (BY LAWFUL MEANS) FORCE THE CHANGES NEEDED!

The European Union:
Its Effect Upon UK Democracy

(Author's note). After completing the first draft of this section, Boris Johnson was appointed as UK prime minster, whose prime intention was to invoke the people's referendum result and exit the EU by the end of October 2019. To his credit, this has now happened. I decided to retain this section mainly unchanged, because of its direct relevance to the importance of a nation's level of true democracy. Also, this 'sensational news' subject continues, and openly demonstrates to me, at least, examples of prejudiced media and the government, contrary to the stated wishes of the people.

* * *

From the outset allow me to declare my own opinion concerning the European Union. It is this. The original idea, called the 'common market' was, in my view, an extremely good concept. A trade agreement amongst member nations which benefited commerce for the member nations and helped make Europe stronger, economically, compared to the USA, the Middle East and the Far East. However, it is not the object of this book to argue either for or against Brexit. But it is entirely relevant to consider the EU's impact upon the level of democracy within the UK. This being, the effect upon the UK's people's amount of influence, in matters of national policies. It is to argue in support of the claim that since the original EU stage of the 'common market', there has been a progressive and serious transfer of UK's governmental powers to a growing bureaucracy in Brussels resulting in a consequential reduction of the democratic rights of UK citizens to influence its own UK Government policies. Let us consider the justification for this point of view.

In this connection, I am indebted to another excellent book written by David Craig and Matthew Elliott entitled *The Great European Rip-Off*, upon 'how the corrupt wasteful EU is taking control of our lives' (Published by Random House Books). This book addresses the question as to whether the EU are constructing a single European super (government) state in which members nation's freedom of action is severely constrained by rules that are formulated by the central EU. Or, is the EU working to deliver a single European market for their common economic benefit (as was originally claimed). To investigate this question the authors, describe six 'treaties' adopted by the EU during the formative years 1957 to

2009. Below is a summary taken from David and Mathews's book, of the changes in national sovereignty and 'self' (national) government.

1. Worryingly, this treaty established increased control over public protection, public health, education and culture. But of serious concern to us in the UK is the Treaty of Rome 1957. This first major treaty was signed by the original six member nations of the new EEC (European Economic Community). It was based upon what was described as 'four freedoms' involving the free movement of goods, services, capital and labour. However, the treaty also set up three powerful institutions, being the European Council, the European Commission and the European Court of Justice. The role and authority of these three institutions gave considerable executive powers over all member nations, at that time. Any regulation issued by the EC automatically became law within the six original nations, resulting in the six nations governments, surrendering their rights to examine, debate or even question any such regulation. The European Court of Justice was given supremacy over all six member nations courts with no rights of appeal. My perspective? This treaty was more to do with the process of transfer of a nation's right of self-government, than the 'four freedoms' defined above. I would also question

how far were the peoples of the six nations consulted about quite a serious transfer of their government's powers to some higher (and less democratic) authority?

2. The Single European Act 1986. By this time, six new nations had joined the EC. Amongst several other treaties and declarations, this particular act delivered the first serious clue about what the EU's real future ambitions were. It was 'claimed' that this act was introduced because 'insufficient progress' had been made towards creating the 'common market' promised by the 1957 treaty. The three European institutions (mentioned above) had cited some 300 measures that, to their minds, needed to be implemented to enable the 'common market' to function as originally proposed. The 'Single European Act' included the transfer of even more powers from member nations to the EC. These were social policy, research and development, environmental standards, and support for the 'poorest' regions. These were labelled 'areas of competence' enabling the EU to regulate in these areas. How these 'areas' are reconciled with increasing progress towards the 'common market' aspect (movement of goods, services, capital and labour) is the subject of serious dispute. One thing is indisputable. It is the continuing transfer of national government powers and authority away

from the nation's own governments and its people. Even more worryingly this act also established the principle for member nations to 'cooperate' on foreign policy and started the process to establish the 'single European currency'. More movement towards a centrally controlled state.

3. The Maastricht Treaty 1991/2. Six years after the Single European Act, this new treaty was brought in. Its intention was to prepare the EU for monetary union and the introduction of the new 'Euro' currency. It set up a timetable for the members nations to 'align' their economic policies in order that the 'Euro' would replace all national currencies by 2002. Even more loss of control was the establishment of the European Central Bank which gave this new financial institution influence in controlling the financial reserves of member nations who adopted the Euro currency. In one single act, those countries lost their right of national economic independence. Happily (for once), both Great Britain and the Republic of Ireland opted out of this deal. All credit to them in this case!

4. The Treaty of Amsterdam. (Here we go again!) This treaty's 'aim' was to remove all border controls between EU countries. Passports were no longer needed to cross borders from one European country to another. Also under this treaty the EU 'fiendishly!' slipped in a transfer of power from member nations to the EU, upon foreign policies which included asylum

policies (e.g. XYZ nation WILL accommodate 50,000 refugees but ABC nation will only need to accept 27!). Also included was employment legislation, and discrimination laws. Finally, this treaty removed a nations right to veto ANY EU policies concerning employment, public health and research. At this point, the authors of *The Great European Rip-Off* delightfully referred to a case where a British MP (I do not know the name) suggested that with the growing reducing workload for the British government, following so much transfer of governmental power to the EU, the number of MPs in the UK Government could be drastically reduced! His political colleagues were not too supportive of this idea!

5. The Treaty of Nice 2001. This treaty's aim was to prepare the EU for enlargement because it planned to allow eastern European nations, together with the Greek part of Cyprus and Malta to join the EU. Sounds reasonable but did this treaty have even more 'hidden and small print' provisions tucked away on 'page 4007' (!) of the text? Yes of course! Why break a habit of a lifetime? This treaty included a 'Charter of fundamental rights (i.e., the right to hold opinions, the right to marry, the right to strike, equality and so on). Sounds OK, but in practical terms it identified a real and serious problem with the whole concept of unifying a large number of separate nations. This is because of the vast amount

of difference in the 'norms, cultures religions, languages and habits' etc. amongst the nations concerned. We have yet to see the consequences of this treaty in practice.

6. The Constitutional Treaty 2004/The Lisbon Treaty 2008/9. Without going into the details of these LAST treatoes (and again using David and Mathews' excellent book), this treaty takes a giant leap in moving to the EU 'super state' because the EU 'elite' wanted to avoid any further treaties which some nations might choose to opt out. In a nutshell it means that any past treaty can be changed without any further consideration by a member nation's own government or their people.

To sum up these six treaties, it is an inescapable conclusion that the nation's powers of self-government, AND their levels of true democracy have been progressively stripped away and transferred to a European bureaucracy. There is simply no substantial argument against this claim. Some 'conspiracy theorists' even argue that the EU development is the 'no war alternative' (by Germany and perhaps France) to rule Europe after failing to achieve this during two world wars! I doubt this myself, but it is a fact that some past 'conspiracy theories' have developed into 'inconvenient truths'.

It is, at the time of writing this book, over three years since the UK's referendum which resulted in a clear (admittedly not overwhelming) majority mandate to leave the EU. How much of the people's own money (public funds) has been used to talk, talk, then talk again with no progress in carrying out 17 million people's wishes. Is this democracy? It is a typical example of how the political elite (from all parties) who do not agree with a majority view of the people conspire to protect their own personal interests and positions by delayed and protracted discussions over a long period of time in the hope of being able to somehow ignore the people's majority view. My perspective was to be extremely suspicious of whatever deal is finally agreed. Too many government responses to 'inconvenient election/referendum results' are likened to redesigning the layout, words and presentation for a packet of washing powder but selling exactly the same product as before!

Again, quoting from David and Mathews' book, referred above, 'some Brussels insiders are even beginning to talk, openly, about what they call a "past democratic age" believing the world is now so complex that it is no longer appropriate to allow (!) ordinary citizens to have a say in how they are governed'. According to them, it is better to leave important decisions to the bureaucratic technocratic elite. Let us recall the historical opposition against democracy, by the words quoted as 'rule by the ignorant and UN-lightened people'. Are we happy with this? If we are, then democracy is indeed dead and buried.

All these foregoing points may sound that I was advocating Brexit. This is NOT the case. As I made clear at the beginning of this section, the original concept of the common market was completely right and should have been developed in accordance with the original concepts but preserving all the nation's rights of self-determination in key democratic principles. Public safety by a defensive pact with a strict definition upon exactly how a European nation would be helped by partner nations if attacked, without reason, by any outside nation. 'Multi-European nation's products, services and developments' for the world's markets. Protection of our nation's borders. Joint educational/scientific research programmes. Health and education cooperation. Progressive improvements to people's standard of living. Protection of every nation's heritage, habits, customs and religions, and so on. In Europe we have, to my mind, the richest and widest collection of talents, abilities and attributes than anywhere else in the world. We have all we need to become an example to the whole world upon how mankind can and should progress which enriches this most beautiful world of ours. It is the PEOPLE of Europe that can do this — by democratic ways.

So, finally, what was the choice for us, the UK people? Without going into the huge amount of information, treaties, views of the media, MPs, banks, European leaders, etc., etc., it was to my mind a very simple question. We already had transferred a large proportion of governmental power to the EU. That is an incontestable fact. If this was to become the permanent situation (following all the buggering about by our leaders) and we stayed in the EU, there is considerably less need for the UK to have its own national government. The House of Commons, with 650 MPs and a considerably large civil service can be drastically reduced ('austerity' cuts for them? Love it!), with the consequential massive savings in public funds. (Could these be somehow paid back to the 'public funds donators' i.e., ourselves). Then we have the House of Lords. No need for them at all. They can go providing even more savings. Now (2023) we have a movement growing to go back into membership. OK, let's have another referendum from the PEOPLE, except this time, let the above question be raised in the referendum. Do I really believe this will happen? We shall see.

So, the simple choice for us the UK people was this. Who do you prefer to be governed by? There is no need for both. By a more democratic 'Westminster'? Or by the growing EU Brussels bureaucracy, with considerably less influence from people in governmental policies throughout Europe?

As we now know, the government, proportions of the media, AND multinational businesses AND major financial institutions, finally capitulated to growing pressure for the national referendum. The 'Brexit Party' was formed, under the leadership of Nigel Farage, to oppose the pressure from the government and commercial 'elite' to remain in the EU. (Throughout this book, I am trying to be completely non-political, but I have to say that if I was asked to name who, in my opinion, was the most democratic political party in the recent past, it would have to be the Brexit Party, later to be named the Reform Party). The fact was that the people of the UK were becoming seriously aware and concerned with the growing power of 'Brussels EU'. A referendum HAD to be held which gave full information and a clear choice of options. A small, yet significant majority wanted 'OUT'. The government, for once, were overruled by the UK people's wishes. This then, represents a clear example of trusting the collective wisdom of the people, after being given full information and a clear choice of options. ('The truth, the whole truth, and nothing but the truth.')

The Growth of Inequality

You may wonder why any growth in inequality in any 'democratic' nation would affect the nation's level of true 'democracy', as we have previously defined. My perspective is that the growth of inequality means that since the 'elite' already has an exceptionally strong influence upon national policies, governmental, commercial or religious, the stronger they are, their current (wholly unsatisfactory) amount of power and influence upon the lives of the overwhelming 'non-elite' classes of a nations populations will grow. People will become increasingly subservient to the elite, without the people realising it! Apart from this 'power factor' factor, there is the aspect of increasing 'propaganda', and distortion of the truth, and the increasing overall (and hidden) abuse of 'power' nationally and internationally. So, logically, if the 'elite' are gaining more and more 'power', where is this element coming from? From us the people, of course!

In this brief chapter upon growing inequality, what evidence is there to define how far this growth really is.

Well, the answer (thankfully) is now available for all of us to see on the web. A report by the United Nations (21st January 2020) upon 'rising inequality', openly states the following.

- 'Inequality' is growing for more than 70% of the global population, exacerbating the risks of divisions and hampering economic and social development. But this rise is far from inevitable, and CAN be tackled at a national and international level.

The report comments that 'the world is confronting the harsh realities of a deeply unequal global landscape in which economic woes, inequalities and job security have led to mass protests in both "developed" and "developing" nations'. And further, 'the study shows that the richest of the population are the big winners in the changing global economy, increasing their share of income (vastly!) between 1990 and 2015' A news item on the web (July 2022) reported the UN secretary as saying that 'Humanity is facing a "perfect storm" of crisis that is widening inequality between the north and the south'. He adds 'the divide is not only morally unacceptable but also dangerous, threatening peace and security in a conflicted world'.

The truth is the UN statement confirms what, precisely, has been happening during the previous decade. In an 'Oxfam' study published in September 2013 entitled

'The true cost of austerity and inequality', it states that in 2012, the World Bank classified the UK as the sixth 'richest' country in the world following socio-economic reforms in the 1980s. 'This shift towards market-based capitalism was characterised by financial liberalisation, the erosion of social security and deregulation of the labour market (e.g., reduction in workers' rights). These reforms led to a dramatic increase in the number of people living in poverty... with inequality reaching levels last seen in the 1920s'!

The 2013 Oxfam report states 'that the UK now (2013) ranks as one of the most unequal countries in the OECD'. A more recent report from Oxfam in 2016 found that around 388 'billionaires' (in the world) owned the same amount of 'wealth' as half the world's population! The incomes of 'working and middle class' workers had stagnated and fallen constantly since 1988, whilst the incomes of the world's wealthiest (the 'elite') had increased substantially.

More recently, in a report by the Institute of Public Policy (November 2019), it is claimed that the UK is amongst the most DIVIDED countries in the 'developed world'. These alarming regional gaps help create economic and political divides. The health, employment, productivity, and disposable income 'divides' are larger than any 'comparable' country.

Of course, this awful truism is not publicised by the media (again), despite it being a grotesquely unfair situation. It demonstrates, yet again, the growing decline in the people's influence upon government and commercial policies. As the report makes clear, this growing unjustified unfairness and inequality IS controllable, if governments are so minded. They clearly have not done this so far, thereby demonstrating the growing level of representativeness of the PEOPLE'S needs, by the nations and world.

So, again by careful research by us 'ordinary unknowing persons', we find out yet another hidden truism that the 'elite' of the world are, firstly becoming even 'richer', and secondly, becoming fewer. I remember seeing some time ago, an ariel view of a palace alongside the Black Sea for the Russian premier. Then a report of the 'medical' services (including the 'pleasure squad') for the Chinese leader and many other such reports. However, more recently I read a report claiming that a former American president had been downgraded from the 'richest 200 in the world'. (Dear, dear, what a shame, how sorry I am!)

If democracy in our world was applied properly, education, health, the environment etc. would become top of the list, paid for by real and proper taxation of the elite classes, for the benefit of humanity, and the whole world environment. As the report clearly confirms, this is NOT an impossible dream, it is quite capable of implementation, if the nations' governments are so willing.

So, let's put these reports to the test for the United Kingdom. To do this I have researched claims of inequality from authoritative sources where accurate and verifiable data is available (rather than 'distorted' propaganda from the current political party in power, or 'reverse' propaganda from the opposition party, not in power). I have rejected some probably accurate claims which may be fully justified and have selected just ten cases for the UK. They are as follows.

- Most schools in the UK will be worse off in real terms, despite funding boosts. Research by the national Education Union found that only 18 out of the 533 Parliamentary constituencies will have real time per pupil funding above the 2015 level. Thirteen of these Parliamentary seats were held by the Conservative Party, currently in power.
- So far as the UK mainland is concerned (England, Scotland and Wales, no disrespect to Northern Ireland), a survey published by 'Resolution Foundation' think tank (July 2019) upon Britain's wealthiest regions, showed that the 'medium family wealth per adult' (property wealth, private pension, financial wealth, possessions) varies *enormously* between the northeast of England (£55,000) and the London/southeast region of England (£176,000). At second highest place is southwest of England (£156,000) compared to the f (£83,000), Wales and

the east Midlands at (£85,000). All the regions lie within about 300 miles from each other.

- In a newspaper article published in March 2020 headed 'Revealed: fund favours the southeast – again' over cities in the north. The fund (£16.5 billion) was set up by the incoming Conservative government to spur new housing development, but it has given far more cash to London and the southeast than to the north England and the Midlands.

- Whilst we are 'having a go' at the London/southeast regions, another statistic was published by none other than HM Customs and Excise in September 2020 on the subject of 'tax avoidance'. This showed London and the southeast to be way ahead of ALL other regions!

- An 'industry study' carried in 2019 found a clear north/ south divide in the performance of manufacturing companies. Investment intentions were classified as 'negative' in the northeast, northwest, east and west Midlands, but industry in the southeast was classified as 'booming'.

- In a newspaper report (January 2020) headed 'Record dividends were paid out during 2019 by UK listed firms' claimed that dividends paid out by companies in the London Stock Exchange to shareholders hit a record 'high', with a total of… (wait for it!) £110.5 million paid out. The same year, average earnings for the 'working classes' dropped in real terms by 1.5%. So, in words (at my level), increases for factory workers, delivery drivers, office staff, hospital workers, teachers, working a five-day week for 52 weeks (being, in my view, the REAL wealth creators), were GROSSLY underpaid, compared to someone sitting down 'playing' on a number of computer screens for a few hours receiving substantially more.

- Then we have the case of the government's national transport policy. In November 2019, the government announced that the cost of London's east/west 'Cross rail' plans will now cost another half a billion pounds and another year's delay from 2020 to 2021. The total estimate at that time was £18.5 billion. At the same time the government announced that the proposed HS2 electric rail line to the Midlands and the north is being 'cut back'. Another case of inequality. But as one newspaper had 'the bottle' to point out, one reason the Conservative Party won the 2019 general election was partially because more constituencies in the Midlands and north voted for the Conservative candidate. How did their MPs vote in this government policy? IN SUPPORT of this these 'inequality' decisions! What might have influenced this action? In my view simply political ambitions rather than representing the voters' wishes, who gave them their vote. Not only does this single incident justify the claims in this chapter, but it also justifies this book's title AND the growing number of books and publications issued by much more knowledgeable and experienced authors than I.

- So far as the government's policies relating to the environment and the UK economy is concerned, we see more examples of local inequality between different regions. In an article in the *Guardian* newspaper (August 2022) headed 'Solar farms refused permission, could have cut bills by £100 million' it is reported that 23 'solar farms' in the UK between January 2021 and July 2022 were affected. This is shocking enough, but when we note that 19 such proposals were in TORY constituencies (who obviously did not want their countryside spoilt by solar panels) we see clear indications of gross inequality and blatant disregard of economic needs. (Levelling up policy? I don't think so.)

- In an article in the 'i' (April 2019) by Janet Street Porter, it was reported that a House of Lords Committee, considering 'intergenerational fairness' (get that for a title!) wanted to drastically prune 'pensioners' perks' (e.g., bus passes, winter fuel allowances etc.), order to give more help to younger people. This is in addition to 'nudging up the pension age'. As Janet rightly said, 'This unelected, very privileged, very highly paid "reward", for past political loyalty, elite body of government is (get this for a truism!) demonising pensioners for not dropping dead sooner'. I have no argument against helping young people more. I say, rather than use the public funds, already paid by the pensioners during their working lives, in income tax, VAT, national insurance, council tax, etc. etc., by slashing the disgraceful level of public funds being wasted by the House of Lords! Well said, Janet!

- Whilst we are on the subject of the 'Upper House' of 'Lords' a more recent article in the *Sunday Times* (July 2022) tells us that the outgoing prime minister attempt to flood the Lords with dozens of new peers could be derailed following the Lord's speaker warnings that such action risks undermining public confidence in our Parliamentary system! (As if they still have any 'public confidence!)

- In another article in the same newspaper (business section), on the same date, a graph is published upon 'inflation and pay' This shows inflation has hit a new high of approaching 10% increase (and is expected to rise even further), compared to 'pay', which has reached a new low of minus 4%, both for 2022. (Further evidence that some newspapers tell us the truth, unlike other politically motivated papers.) In May 2022, the UK's government cabinet sent out a clear directive that all public sector workers are required to show restraint in wage demands. This despite soaring inflation and cost of living. This from the government 'cabinet' comprising, virtually, of all millionaires!

- In a paper published in December 2019 by the Office for National Statistics entitled 'Country and Regional Public Sector Finances', it is reported:

1. London, the southeast and the east of England, all had 'net' fiscal gap between total spending and revenue (e.g., tax raised) surpluses in the financial year 2019, with ALL other regions in the UK having NET fiscal deficits.

2. London raised the most revenue per head at £18,195 in the year ending 2019, while Wales and the northeast raised the least per head, the northeast raised the least per head at £9,409 and £9,533 respectively. But this is also, additional proof of wholesale inequality in earnings, between the regions.

3. In an article in the *BBC Focus* magazine (April 2020) it was reported that the UK Court of Appeal ruled that the UK Government's decision to approve a new third runway at Heathrow Airport was illegal as it breached its own policy commitments under the 2015 PARIS agreement on climate change. A clear example in my view, of the government, 'leaning over backwards' in favour of the London/southeast region.

To summarise, London, the southeast and east England received much more money than it needed (through higher wages principally, not exclusively), where all other regions had less revenue, but needed more total spending.

FINALLY

Going back again to the year 2019, an article in one of the more responsible morning papers headed 'Bank chief earns £6.4 million as bank branches are axed'. Another seriously alarming example of both selfish, OBSCENE inequality and the power of the 'elite'. I quote this final report because, in my view, the circumstances are outrageously selfish inequality. To quote the report. 'The banking group Santander, which last month announced 140 branch closures and tumbling profits, has revealed that its 'boss' was paid £6.4 million salary and bonuses LAST YEAR (2018). This was made up by his annual salary of £1.7 million, then £638.000 benefits, AND finally £1.8 million to "compensate" him for the share bonuses he "gave up" when he left RBS Bank, who needed (OUR) public money for the bank to avoid bankruptcy, to join Santander.'

To sum up, from this report. He was paid a total of £6.4 million pounds in one year, during which the bank's UK profits had fallen by 14%, AND the bank had been 'fined' £33 million for 'serious failings' in processing deceased customers' accounts, AND a total of about 1,200 jobs are 'at risk' from the 140 branches being closed.

Serious inequality? I call it criminal inequality, but apparently that is the kind of world we live in. I just wonder what a few 'criminals' serving prison sentences for, say, stealing £5,000 from the employer, might say about inequality if they knew about this case. PERHAPS WE SHOULD REWARD THEM TOO FOR THEIR PAST FAILINGS!

If all these claims are true it is a most serious indictment that all the previous paragraphs in this chapter are absolutely justified. If any of the foregoing is untrue or unjustified, I offer my unreserved apology, by stating that I am only referring to a past fully published, national newspapers report. I do not believe for one moment the latter case arises.

As was stated in the opening paragraph of this chapter, the growing rise in inequality CAN be tackled if governments are so minded. What is happening today? The UK Government has brought in a new policy, entitled 'Levelling Up'. Basically, this means giving more public funds to areas deemed to be less provided for (my interpretation). Fine words, or more 'politic speak'? Let us carefully monitor the actual consequences of this proposed policy in terms of truthful and verifiable facts, rather than more 'politic speak' issued by the government in power, but, again, by a professional, non-political, independent association. (Watch this space!) 'Levelling up?' We shall see in time.

So, finally, let's put this 'levelling up policy' to the test, using accurate figures quoted on the web. Firstly, wages for the working population. The annual average wage for the current year (2022) is estimated at £24,600. This can be divided to an hourly rate of £12.80p (i.e., 52 weeks, 37 hours. weekly). The average wage for the previous year was £25,971, showing a reduction of the national average wages figure of 5%. (Let's not forget cost of living increases!) How does this compare to MPs average income over a similar period? According to Wikipedia, as of April 2022, the average pay for MPs is £84,144, an increase of about 2.7% from the previous year. BUT this figure does not include expenses. For 2021 the average paid expenses for MPs were £157,747, for the year, 'up an inflation busting average of 6.5% on the year before' (quote). Finally in a survey published by 'Resolution Foundation' (June 2022) this showed my own beloved city, Nottingham, has the lowest disposable income in the whole of the UK. Meanwhile London (you've guessed it!) is the 'richest', enjoying more than four times the disposable income of the poorest parts of the UK. If we 'levelled this UP', we would need to increase average earning by 7.5% PLUS, issuing cost of living support (for housing, food etc., etc.) 6.5% for all workers! More of this in Chapter 12.

Information Technology

The inequality, abuse and effect upon democracy.

(Note) From the outset, dear reader, I must warn you that this chapter will take some reading. It is, in my view, one of the most important characteristics of the decline in national and worldwide democracy, which, again, to my mind, is of equal importance to the world's environmental crisis. So please, persevere and read every part of this chapter. It is a growing and hidden crisis that, in my view, threatens the whole world's future.

A short time ago, whilst drafting one of the chapters in this book, I was chatting to an old friend of mine (from 'academic' times), about democracy decline, and he suddenly suggested I consider a growing viewpoint that developing information technology has similar characteristics to a worldwide commercial 'war' scenario, detrimental to mankind. 'No way Jose!' was my response, 'look at all the benefits,' I said. I then came across an article (in one of the more 'responsible' newspapers. I cannot recall which) that argued that we, the people, really are becoming caught up in this 'war'.

This is caused, it was claimed, by thousands of 'IT' organisations constantly in intense competition with each other, developing and changing IT characteristics, both hardware and software, literally daily, without any control, whatsoever. This applies to all forms of IT therefore, it is becoming more important to keep abreast of these changes, despite the many benefits (and information) of this technology. As with all 'wars', it is only we, the people, that suffer and must pay for the consequences. So, worth checking out this claim.

Firstly, let us remind ourselves what is meant by 'transparency' in relation to 'information'. In my Collins Dictionary, the defining words appropriate to the subject of this book are 'clarity', 'clearness', 'explicitness' and 'undisguised'. A 'Wikipedia' definition on the web states 'transparency, as used in business, humanities and social contexts, is operating in such a way, that it is easy for others to see what actions are performed. Transparency implies openness, communication and accountability'. Wikipedia goes on to clarify 'In politics, transparency is used as a means of holding public officials (MPs councillors and public service officers) accountable' and finally 'participative democracy is more closely connected to the will of the people'. In all these and other definitions, it surprises me a little with the absence of words like 'all information' (completeness), 'nothing excluded', consistently easy for ALL people to understand, and similar standards. No matter. The meaning is clear enough for us to judge how 'transparency' should be, in today's real-life circumstances. We can also apply our own interpretation of the opposite of 'transparency'. My perspective? 'The distortion, concealment and untruthful description of important and relevant information'. This second interpretation is of serious relevance to the whole subject of democracy, locally, nationally and worldwide.

Within the (to my mind, 'excellent') magazine *BBC Science Focus* (March 2021) is an outstanding article, written by none other than the inventor of the world wide web, Professor Sir Tim Berness-Lee, in 1989. All credit to Professor Sir Tim for creating a wonderful innovation designed originally for the open communication and exchange of academic research work from worldwide universities. Tremendous value was made available by developing information technology. Alas, entering this brilliant innovation over the years has been exploitive, unrestrained commercialism and politics (the pursuit of profit and power). Result? To quote Sir Tim's summary headline. 'The rise of disinformation, online abuse, and extremism has shown the web is not the glowing network of knowledge, community and togetherness we once hoped it could be.' Worldwide abuse and exploitation of privacy, and the excessive influence upon people opinions and actions, where the most detailed information upon people's lifestyle is known, circulated and SOLD worldwide. The old concept of 'Big Brother is watching YOU' has now become absolute reality, again, of 'crisis' proportions. To my mind the whole purpose and objective of 'information technology' is now the increasing influence upon our lives, views and attitudes, for the benefit of power acquisition for 'the few'. As a well-qualified 'IT' friend of mine once said 'the real objective of "Silicon Valley" is simply world domination!'

One of the most important kinds of inequality in any nation (democratic or non-democratic) is the subject of 'public' information. That is, how much the people of a nation are given, compared to how much a nation's leadership has. The reason is, again, quite simple. The need to acquire and hold on to 'power' and 'authority' can only be achieved by having considerably more information than that held by the people of a nation, OR by opposing parties seeking to gain power and authority for themselves. This is where I, and many, many others claim serious inequality arises between the nation's leaders and 'us' the people.

Possession of that 'resource' or commodity, means a nations leadership can use it, to retain and extend their power, authority and control. Put another way, only information which can be used (or 'adjusted') to favourably impress and influence people's views and opinions will be published and emphasised. Information which identifies fault, criticism or causes alarm or reduced confidence/trust, for a current leadership is kept secret. Additionally, it can be used and 'adjusted' to lay blame upon others seeking to acquire power themselves, or by claiming external influences over which the current leadership can argue 'not our fault'. I personally sum this up simply. It is the 'politicisation' of public information by a nations governmental leaders which urgently needs appropriate controls, to protect us from being influenced in our views, by these actions.

The warnings about 'disinformation' go back many years. Even past nation's leaders acknowledged it! At the end of the Second World War, when the dreadful atrocities committed by the German Nazi troops in Poland's concentration camps were exposed, the American President Eisenhower gave an order along the following lines. 'Take as many photographs of these dreadful scenes of piles of dead bodies as you can, and obtain and safely store, all documentary evidence that you can find, because you can be bloody sure that someone in the future will try to argue that this never happened.' Yet again, the wisdom and warnings from the old, yet enlightened people being ignored and (conveniently to some) forgotten.

I take much interest in what our politicians say publicly through the media. Ignoring, for the moment, the media's excessive thirst for 'scoop sensations', it is not too difficult to see from what is said that their worded responses are all carefully 'pre planned'. Specific words, clarified by 'IT specialists' as being effective forms of propaganda are used, not to clarify a situation, but to influence the people's perspective. To use a quote from another excellent past book *The Silent State*, by Heather Brooks, this tactic is defined very accurately as 'taxpayer subsidised propaganda'. Heather's book accurately clarifies situations occurring some 10/12 years ago, but it clearly demonstrates the serious absence and inequality of 'transparency' at that time. It is even more serious today as will be seen in the following pages. As a 'political' friend of mine (yes, I do have some!) once told me, there are two vitally important principals to observe in 'politic speak'. Firstly, it is essential to describe the circumstances of any national situation, whether good or bad, in a way that improves the image of the ruling party. Secondly, it is more important to appear to be doing something (talk, talk), than actually doing nothing!

Do please listen, very carefully, to senior politicians giving TV and media interviews, as we currently had, during the coronavirus disaster. Every answer to every question will be to give 'positive' responses about what the current administration IS doing or INTENDS to do in the immediate future. Little is said about how this problem occurred in the first place, and how the responses will actually deal with the problem, OR whether there may be negative consequences of the actions if any 'self-fault' might become apparent. At the time of writing, the effects of the coronavirus disaster is the subject of considerable political statements, but evidence is finally coming to light of the UK Government repeatedly ignoring many past authoritative warnings of this pandemic, keeping this quiet and doing nothing to deal with a growing, very serious, problem. As another test, you could listen to, or read about their responses and look for any admission of self-fault which would, at least demonstrate openness and an element of honesty. I fear you will find very little. As mentioned above the 'fallback option' is to lay blame on others. (Politicians who are 'skilful'(!) in this kind of 'talent', get promoted to senior roles!) It is far better to tell what the ruling party thinks the people want to hear, than admitting the presence of 'bad news'. Remember, whatever situation arises, 'good or bad' political policy statements will be grammatically worded to show the governing party in the best light and will hide many 'inconvenient truths'. Blaming others (May 2020), US President Trump had an outstanding 'talent'. He has repeatedly said the blame for not having stockpiles of crucial medical supplies for the forthcoming pandemic lies with his predecessor Barrack Obama *ignoring documentary evidence to prove otherwise*. Clearly, someone ought to remind the (past) US president that the people are the masters of the nation, and they pay (through taxation), and hire public servants and elected representatives to govern in accordance with the people's wishes. *Is this not mentioned in the American constitution?*

Every single day, computers are making more and more decisions affecting everybody's lives, than we realise. A simple example is in today's methods of recruitment. Applications for employment are now required only via the web. Are they then considered by a recruitment manager? No, a software package examines your input document searching for the use of 'keywords'. If a reasonable amount is located by the software, the applicant is selected for interview, with little in the way of looking at the full application by reading the whole presentation. I am looking forward to the day when a male applicant, having been selected for interview by a computer, for a senior appointment, turns up for interview wearing a Saxon war helmet, stockings and suspenders and football boots! Do please let me know dear reader WHEN this happens! (NB. He/she would NOT get the job!)

An article in the magazine *Science Focus* (summer 2022) addresses two very important questions. Are 'remote workers' less productive? And can remote workers communicate effectively? This article makes the point that 'modern technology' (IT), still cannot replicate all the rich and subtle cures that 'face to face' communication involves. Whilst I do not understand the answers to these questions, I still ask, 'which is more intelligent, the best IT system currently being used – OR the power of the human brain?' This very informative article follows extensive studies published in 2021 in native human behaviour, which showed negative consequences upon communications and team performance when some or all employees worked 'remotely'. My view as a fully qualified 'computer dummy', ordinary citizen, is simple. The human brain is infinitely better than computers, today AND the future. Not convinced? Take some time and read authoritative descriptions upon the amazing capabilities of the human mind, which includes so much more than any computer. Things like compassion for others, love, intuition, lessons from history, justice for all, protection of the planet and its environment, and so on.

The 'inequality' aspect of transparency mentioned above is one vitally important factor of democracy. On the one hand people are being constantly denied access to vital, important and relevant information at the same time as the nation's leadership (and the 'elite' in society) gain more and more information about us, the people, from whom comes all the governments funds resources. ('He who pays the piper, calls the tune?' I think not!) My perspective? Transparency is becoming grossly unequal and a 'one-way ticket' in favour of a nation's elite and leadership.

A key aspect of having a true democracy in any nation is that citizens actively participate in politics and civic life. This means that people have an unreserved right to be informed about all public matters; to know how, truthfully, the government is using its powers (and OUR money). The people are thus able to express better opinions and preferences upon various important issues. Let's take just one recent example demonstrating that this is NOT happening. In January 2020, the UK Department of Health and Social Care claimed that 18 NEW hospitals had opened during the past 10 years (a period of rule by one political party). However, further investigations revealed that this figure included refurbished and redeveloped existing hospitals. These are NOT 'new' hospitals! The current governments manifesto pledges to build 40 new hospitals over the next 10 years. Pity, the original claim did not really materialise. If this had happened, we may not have found it necessary to call in the armed forces and voluntary helpers to supplement our public health services during the coronavirus crisis. The discrete and hidden 'commercialisation' of medical and healthcare services would be, then, clearly seen. This is another example of distortion of the facts concerning an essential public service for which the majority of people have already paid for, in their 'national insurance' contributions. The government knew what the people were concerned about in the past (e.g., The evidence of queues of emergency ambulances waiting outside hospitals before the occurrence of the coronavirus crisis), failed to respond to this situation, and finally issued distorted information to the people. How does the government reconcile past extensive cutbacks (e.g., Health, police etc., etc.), during 'austerity' policies and then, suddenly, promise to build 40 new (!) hospitals in the next 10 years. And this is without considering the future unknown, but enormous cost, of dealing with the final consequences of the coronavirus crisis. In all the government statements concerning the spread of this dreadful disease, government spokesmen repeatedly keep telling us what to do (e.g., 'distancing etc.'), and then go on to warn us of the legal consequences (breaking 'laws' and immediate heavy fines). Of course, we now see (March 2022) such laws should not apply to the 'elite' levels e.g., the government, who actually laid down the laws of 'distancing' in the first place!, At last, we see a rare sign of real equality. WELL DONE to the police force! And how will this threat be 'policed' anyway particularly when the truth is that less than 50% of all reported crime cannot be dealt with because of lack of police resources. Another public service needing more investment. Or are we going to 'commercialise' this service as well?

Again, if we listen to all the promises coming from the current and past governments, about helping the unemployed, helping businesses, as well as providing 40 'new' hospitals, we might ask ourselves where is all this money suddenly coming from? I can give you the answer. From YOU, during the next (say) four generations, considering the nation's current financial situation. One thing we can do is to start to demand, from official independent sources accurate information upon our national debt, with responsible comments about the causes and a prediction upon how long this situation is going to prevail. If this could be successfully achieved – and openly published – we are not going to like the answers! This is happening all the time. How can we expect people to give a reasonable and fair judgement during elections and referendums, when they are subjected to 'propaganda' types of 'information', either from government sources, prejudiced media or 'pursuit of profit ONLY' commercial organisations?

This growing 'obscenity' of inequality of transparency is finally becoming obvious both in the public sector and also in the private and commercial sector. In a newspaper article (January 2020) arising from an interview with a retiring senior civil servant, the extent of data held by the 'private sector' was described as way more information and data about any of 'us' (the people), than MI5 ('secret service') would ever have about individuals. Whilst our need for our nation's defences to have extensive confidential information about all relevant matters cannot really be questioned, the fact is that we are becoming a more 'one-sided transparency nation'. Government and commercial organisations can acquire and store enormous amounts of information about 'us' the people, but we (the people) have increasingly less access to real and accurate information about government actions and the commercial data banks that do a roaring trade in selling data about us to other commercial organisations, without our specific knowledge or consent. The level of surveillance in the UK is universally regarded as one of the highest in the world. I can recall at least two personal experiences of this uncontrolled transparency 'inequality'. I pay for 'Netflix' on my TV, principally for watching films, documentaries and humorous programmes. I am now receiving emails from Netflix advising me of films like those previously watched. How did they get my email address and what data is being stored and computed concerning my interests? And, is this data being 'sold' on to other organisations without my knowledge? I am now receiving emails from media newspapers urging me to take out a subscription for regular daily issues. How was my email address, my computer 'ID' and interests passed onto them? I certainly did not. Information technology is a wonderful facility. Used properly, it advances the positive progress of mankind considerably. But it is also a dangerous weapon. July 2020 on the web, 'Twitter' says, about 130 'accounts' were targeted in one week. 'Hackers' had accessed internal data systems to hijack some of the top 'voices' in the USA.

So, once again, being reluctant to accept these claims, I carried out a test of my own, some time ago. Firstly, from news reports on the web, I selected a few upon various news reports, and highlighted the entry for more information. In many cases, I was only shown the first page of the article. The remaining part was progressively faded out. Up came a message ('outrageously') making the claim 'Your privacy is important to us'. This goes on to say your interest can be passed onto organisations which are relevant to the subject of my enquiry. You are given a choice, EITHER 'Accept' this arrangement OR you can be given 'further information'. (NOTE, you are not given the option of replying 'no thank you'.) So, I chose the option 'more information'. Up comes a whacking big list of hundreds of organisations, worldwide, to whom my interest may be passed, together, presumably, with my name and 'IT' contact information. 'My privacy is important?'! I do not think so. More on this subject later. (Another somewhat more light-hearted incident related to a friend of mine with whom we were having a laugh about the 'Alexa' service and some of the daft questions that are being asked over the phone. Then, after a pause, he asked, 'I don't suppose Alexa is keeping a record of our somewhat 'questionable' questions?'). BE WARNED dear reader, be warned!

Yes, of course, there must be certain types of government information which have to be classified as legitimately secret, and commercial organisations need to have extensive and accurate marketing information to stay in business. But, once again, I repeat, every freedom must have basic, reasonable and fair constraints. Lessening transparency for the people upon many aspects of their lives, needs and interests, increases lack of trust and confidence in both government and commerce. Just having 'edited' versions of the truth or having no verifiable facts at all will cause people to have less justified opinions and impressions about important matters. One of the most important messages I want to try to get across is in this book is 'trust the collective judgements and wisdom of people, upon vitally important issues' but they MUST be given full and accurate information, which includes 'inconvenient truths' in order for the people to give a proper response. One of the consequences of the reducing levels of transparency is the growth of 'conspiracy theories' which we should consider. For now, let us emphasise the question. 'Do we, the people, not have the right to access much more factual information before national and global catastrophic events arise?' (Or elections!) Transparency HAS to be a two-way deal. The people's growing distrust of governments and the growth of 'conspiracy theories' come about because of lack of information, distortion of information, irrelevant information and downright lies.

A brief article in a UK national newspaper (August 2020) headed 'UK behind the curve, on Russian meddling', reported that the UK is ('behind') the curve in preventing political interference from Russia. It was claimed that the UK is 'wholly inadequate' in deterring and responding to Russian activity. If true, here we have another international example of governments (UK and Russia) using IT for purely political gain purposes, rather than getting on with the job of dealing with the world's real problems. On the very same page, a brief report states that the number of confirmed coronavirus cases in Africa has passed the one million level, but that the real toll is probably several times higher! It later turns out to be, in truth, much LESS. Clearly political leaders are simply saying 'don't bother about that, how can we score a few more political points against (XYZ) but keep it low profile!'

Being somewhat of a 'science fiction' addict, the matter of 'flying saucers' and 'alien beings' from other worlds' attracts my ('warped?') interest. But I try to keep a balanced view on this whole subject. It seems to me however (my 'perspective') that I cannot ignore all the many claims that 'flying saucers' do exist and (probably) 'aliens' of a much higher knowledge and intelligence than ours monitor and even influence the development of mankind, and (hopefully) the protection of this beautiful planet of ours. There are just too many knowledgeable scientists, people of repute, senior politicians and professional researchers raising legitimate questions about past and present events to ignore the possibility that some of these claims are probably true. Is this not therefore a matter of serious concern to us the people? Just the possibility that nations' leaders (political, military, dictators, religious, commerce, etc.) again, have information on this matter which they deny to us, is an absolutely hideous crime of 'anti-transparency' by the 'elite' in the whole history of mankind. If these theories turn out to be the truth, sometime in the future, I trust and hope that the former 'anti-transparency' elite are named and shamed and brought to justice for possessing extremely highly important information which the people of this planet have a right to know.

Finally on this aspect I hope and pray that perhaps truly benevolent aliens of a much higher level of intelligence are caring for our planet, mankind and all other lifeforms and aspects of our world, rather than some of the evil, insane and greedy leaders of our nations. If you want to see examples of 'conspiracy theories', watch a Netflix documentary entitled 'Unacknowledged'.

Turning onto another aspect of 'transparency inequality', we can now give a reasonably accurate overview of the whole European Union experience. When, in 1975, the people voted in a referendum to join the 'common market' (as it was originally called), we had much more of the truth, facts and reality of what was in store for us, under the proposals then in force. Given these facts, the people voted to join, and this was a correct decision because of the circumstances that existed at that time. (Another example of 'trust the people to give the right decision after being giving all the facts'!) In their defence, neither the government nor the people could know, at that time how the 'common market' would change during the following years. Chapter 7 defines how the ensuing 'treaties' progressively transferred whole chunks of the nation's democratic power to determine its own government policies to the now named 'European Union'. It is all too easy to criticise past actions after the event has occurred. Anyone can do that. I ask those that have this habit to accurately predict a future event. Then they become somewhat silent. Finally in respect of the EU the truth emerged and despite political and media attempts to influence people's opinions, the people, on two occasions, voted to leave. Now that the UK is out of the EU, what of the future? I appreciate this is impossible to know. What I do expect is more openness and increased transparency from the UK Government, even if things go wrong. For 'Pete's sake' give the truth, good or bad, and trust the people. We will have much more trust in a government if they have 'the bottle' to openly accept mistakes of their own making, give the truth, and then propose remedies. As these transfers of power (mentioned previously) were taking place, I personally do not recall much (if any) information being published either by the government or the media, that this was happening. Information of this kind should have been openly given out upon such important changes to enrich the 'collective wisdom of the people'. True democracy has many benefits and the consensus views of the people (given all the facts) upon vitally important issues should be respected.

As mentioned previously, there are exceptions to every rule and the need for increased transparency is no different. For example, the Justice and Security Act 2013 introduced 'statutory closed material procedures' which refers to material that could damage national security. Under the Terrorism Act 2000, certain extreme terrorist organisations are listed ('proscribed') which, again, acceptably, excludes the provision of some rights of transparency. There will be others where the exception is perfectly acceptable. It is all the many other government policies where the problem is. Collins Dictionary again gives yet more clarification of transparency, 'that (which) can be seen through distinctly'. The opposite of transparency, in my view, would be 'distortion and concealment of important information'. Yet another quote comes from the USA acts of democratic law. 'People are the masters of the country and they hire public servants and elect their government representatives and pay their taxes. They (the people) are thus totally entitled to know what their public servants (and representative governments) are doing.' It is no excuse to say that consultations and communications with ALL people upon all government matters is an impossibly large task. Information technology is now so advanced that this 'excuse' becomes more and more unjustified as is clearly evidenced by the colossal amount of information obtained by the government and commerce, as mentioned earlier upon us, the people.

It is a sad reflection upon all the governments of the world, supported as they are, by so much technology and science research (and public money), that it takes one internationally respected naturalist David Attenborough, and a former US vice president, Al Gore ('inconvenient truths') to warn the people of the world of a growing crisis arising from climate change and the abuse of our world's environment. Are not their warnings of the collapse of civilisation and the growing levels of extinction of much of the natural world, the duty of nations' leaders and governments to identify openly and then take actual firm and drastic action (rather than 'talk, talk') to deal with these dreadfully serious issues? To use just one example of hundreds, perhaps thousands of scientifically proved examples of how mankind is (without realising it) killing the natural world, I quote again, from another authoritative source, the BBC's *Science Focus* magazine. This reports that the amount of 'plastic pollution' is becoming seriously problematical in the oceans. At least 700 species including sharks, whales, seabirds and turtles are becoming entangled in plastic, or mistake it for a tasty snack because of food etc. residues on the plastic. David Attenborough is quoted as saying to the UN, 'the world's people have spoken, their message is clear. Time is running out. The people want YOU, the decision makers, to be more open and act NOW.' What was one immediate response from one world leader? To pledge his nation will withdraw from the 'Paris Accord' on curbing greenhouse gases, despite nearly every other government, at least, demanding action. He dismissed (the report says) projections from his own government advisers that climate change will seriously affect his nation's economy. My perspective? Bugger the economic aspect, that will not last long anyway in a derelict world! To him and other 'world leaders' I say, 'get off your high horse, and get on with what the people say'!

Turning again to the Brexit matter, from the 'transparency' aspect. I defined in Chapter 7, the various treaties which progressively transferred a variety of the member nations' government powers to the EU at Brussels. Like many of us at that time I took little interest in this activity, and I recall that little attention was given to these changes in the media. Consequently, we, the people, were not aware of these vitally important losses of our own governments powers. Again, government/political/commercial independent people started to raise questions. They were vilified initially, but as the debate went on, the truth began to emerge. But this did not stop politicians, commercial leaders and some sections of the media from extolling the 'virtues' and 'benefits' of EU membership. We should not forget the appallingly long and protracted debates by the UK Government and the bullying tactics of EU leaders. Nor should we forget that the then 'speaker' of the House of Commons, John Bercow had 'the bottle' to say that a 'contempt of Parliament' had been committed by the failure to publish relevant legal advice concerning Brexit. This was later confirmed to be completely true. All credit to Mr Bercow. (He was 'replaced' shortly after. Surprise, surprise!). 'Transparency?' I don't think so. We need more 'John Bercows' in government. Not less.

A friend of mine, with whom I was discussing the declining level of transparency in the whole world, asked me the question, 'Are there many really secret places in the world about which the people knew little or nothing?' My first impression was that there were some but not many, given that modern technology and communication would at least identify the few that exist. However, good question. So, I carried out a web search. I was astonished to see a colossal list. The following is an extracted version.

The Vatican Archives.

Area 51 in the USA.

Terracotta Warriors China (closed area).

Metatheory Town. Russia Closed to the public.

Mount Weather Emergency Operations Centre Severely restricted area.

Fort Knox USA ('gold' stocks). Severely restricted access.

Mormon Church Secret Vault USA. Shinto Ground Shrine Japan (Religious sites).

Secret/laboratories, USA/Russia. (Claimed to be related to 'alien' matters.)

What are the 'excuses' for denying the world's population the truth behind these (and many others) facilities? In my perspective, it can only be for the one principal reason. Protection of 'power' for the world's 'elite', whether they be political, commercial, religious, dictatorial or military. There are far too many secret facilities in our world, where we (the people) have no control whatsoever. This, even though US ('the unwashed, unclean, ignorant, masses') actually pay for many, if not all, of these secret places. We need to demand justification for these secrets by establishing a 'people's policy', which limits the circumstances where (our) public money is used to establish these areas. The important thing is that people are not as stupid, irresponsible and untrustworthy as the elite choose to believe.

I recall that not so long ago, the organisation 'transparency international' who maintains a listing of the most and least transparent nations in the world (180 nations), reported that the UK had dropped three places to be outside the top ten. The US fell six places in the index and Azerbaijan dropped 30 places. Denmark and Sweden scored the highest points. Is this not yet more proof that transparency 'downwards' (from the 'elite' to the people) IS reducing? The typical 'excuse' (to some degree only) is 'public safety'. Whilst transparency 'upwards', from people to the 'elite' is a different story all together. In an excellent article entitled 'Look out, we are being watched' ('i' newspaper 26th February 2019) the writer records that the UK is one of the most "watched" nations in the world. Six million cameras (at that time!) follow our every move, from home to work, out drinking with friends, playing with children, and attending social (and sporting) events. Add to this that every time you use your mobile phone, open your 'tablet/kindle', send emails, use Facebook etc., etc., you are often being monitored, both within the law and, sadly, more often, outside the law. Every time you pay a shopping bill, using your store card, use a 'bus pass', your actions are being recorded and (most worryingly) analysed and very often 'sold on' to other organisations you have probably never heard of before. (Open your laptop and go onto the news items, and a little message, on the screen, admits this.) CCTV images are recorded from all kinds of sources, including social media, police body cameras, transport, public events are in constant use. To which, I would add, even the 'dustbin emptying vehicles' are now constantly recording the frontage of every house visited! The lines between state and private surveillance are being 'blurred'. Are we not worried yet?! All credit to organisations such as the Civil Rights Group for trying to champion the people's interests. BUT THEY AND OTHER SIMILAR organisations AND THE PEOPLE ARE NOT BEING TAKEN NOTICE OF!

Information technology, therefore, is being used to undermine democratic processes, rather than facilitate them. 'Fake news', unrestricted populist messages, computer hacking, and 'cyber warfare' from rival nations are just some of the known abuses of IT. Is it being so paranoic to think that whilst I am writing up this chapter, in some way, I am being 'monitored?' For the time being

I will believe 'not'. However, do I recall correctly that a bill has been passed by HM government, giving intelligence services sweeping powers of surveillance, including tools for 'snooping' and 'hacking?' These provide more methods for political regression. These warnings about IT are increasingly coming from so many different directions. A web report from the *Independent* newspaper in September 2020 was headed 'British military facing a modern day "blitz" with 60 cyberattacks a day'. With the means to carry out operations which degrade, disrupt and destroy critical capabilities and infrastructure. Cyberspace has the means to interfere in our democratic rights and processes. The above statement (cyberattacks) originated from a very senior UK military commander!

Let us consider more whether information technology is affecting the basic principles of democracy. Again, we must always keep reminding ourselves of the many, many benefits that IT brings to literally every aspect of humankind and our beautiful world. Medical science, clean energy, food production, 'people' benefits, and many, many more. This work must be protected, properly managed and developed. My fears about the growing faults and misuse of information technology would not be justified or fair without an unreserved acknowledgement of the THOUSANDS of benefits to the world and the environment derived from information technology systems. Just by way of ONE example from millions, I quote from an article in the *Guardian* newspaper in May 2023. Headline: 'Brain machine helps a paralysed man to walk using wireless signals'. Comment from the patient? 'For the first time in 10 years, I was able to stand up and have a beer with my friends. That was pretty cool!' But is there a growing and serious hidden danger in 'IT'? How far, really, does this technology control our very existence and democratic rights, without our realising it? The answer is that there is the beginning (thankfully) of many claims by authoritative and knowledgeable sources, who have carried out impressive levels of research, that 'IT' has an increasing and serious 'dark side', which we are only recently being told about. Not by the world's leaders, who simply abuse, distort and 'edit' information in order to gain, retain and increase their powers. In another excellent, yet alarming book, entitled 'The people VR's tech.', written by one of the world's leading experts on 'the digital revolution' (author James Bartlett), the growing dangers of 'IT' are now becoming well defined clearly, how we all use these facilities is being exploited and abused by thousands of different organisations, without our knowledge or consent. James clarifies that when he refers to 'technology', he means digital technology i.e., Data/Information technology, e.g., 'Silicon Valley'. This would include laptops, mobile phones, store cards, bank cards, stores cards, bus passes (our beloved 'Alexa'!) and so on. James very well defines how this type of technology is increasingly dominating economic, political and social aspects of our very existence. As an ordinary citizen, I did not appreciate that 'democracy' (however we choose to interpret this word), and 'digital technology' have 'wholly different fundamental principles and basic concepts', to quote one of James's principal conclusions. This raises a most serious question as to how far 'IT' has reduced important elements of democracy (rule by the people, for the people), and acquired increasing control and influence in matters of serious concern to individual people, communities, nations and indeed, the whole world. As an example question, how far did 'IT' originally influence the developing use of 'plastics' throughout the world? We now know the global disaster that has occurred in our oceans. Could it be, for instance, that 'IT' contributed to this problem in the first place? By showing that increasing the use of plastics materials would considerable decrease production costs, create cheaper prices for the customer and more profits for the suppliers? Effect in the environment? No, sorry. That was not in the programme's software!

This is why I argue that information technology MUST be 'policed' and claimed 'benefits' to be thoroughly 'audited'. The cost of doing this? It would be paid for by a worldwide 'IT tax' on 'Silicon Valley' and similar associations (they can well afford this!) paid to a specialist independent police force, managed by an elected non-political public body (supported by independent specialists) whose roles would be clearly defined

The whole business and objectives of 'social media' (Google, Facebook, Twitter etc., etc.,) is (it is claimed) to give a free service of data information to users (like myself) in literally any subject we choose to be interested in. But it is increasingly NOT free! Because in exchange for this service, we are being 'watched' and 'recorded' somewhere, somehow. As already shown, this collective data is then, again, without our knowledge or consent, being sold on to a whole host of different agencies who sell this data, including personal information about ourselves, on to a whole host of different organisations (both government and commercial) for their uncontrolled use by 'decision makers'. This helps in the new 'science' of identifying significant 'wordology' (i.e., 'politic speak') which is most effective in influencing people's opinions, attitudes and preferences, in a wide and specific variety of different ways. They use this data for their own benefit whether it is for illegal activities, political gain, commercial profit ('don't worry about the oceans!') or just decreased control of us, the 'ill-informed and unwashed' ordinary people! Further proof that information confers power to the 'elite'.

In my view, what is urgently needed (NOW) is firstly for new 'criminal' laws to be drawn up, clearly identifying the specific growing list of abuses by today's information technology. We can no longer trust our governments to do this. There is simply far too much 'personal interests' (direct or indirect), being regularly ignored. NO! This list can only be drawn up by an independent, non-political, professional, academic, legal judicial group, with a people's national jury. They would clearly identify new illegal practices and the laws and punishments needed to outlaw information technology abuses. The report would be openly published for all to see, and the government in power at the time would be required to hold a national referendum where the main political parties would publish their own manifestos showing HOW they would introduce the report's conclusions. The result of the referendum would finally become mandatory for the incoming/current government to introduce immediately without the past habit of 'delaying tactics'.

So, to finalise this most seriously worrying aspect of democracy, 'IT' is a wonderful facility for everyone, but fundamental standards must be more regularly reviewed and enforced, again by independent, non-political, non-commercial professional bodies who have the sole responsibility, enshrined by statute, of protecting the people's interests only. To put the final sentence of this chapter. 'I am entitled to have appropriate levels of privacy AND as much information about the "Elite" (as previously defined), as they have about me. I am entitled to have all sides of the story'. And this applies to ALL people.

Unfortunately, the reality of what 'information technology' really means is overwhelmed by commercial activity ('sell, sell, sell'), and an appalling/increasing DEARTH of INFORMATION (real news, truisms, events and facts).

Finally, let me pose questions about two real dangers arising from increasing reliance upon information technology. Firstly, can the human brain itself, advance its abilities and powers EQUALLY with the growth and complexity of information technology? (I say 'YES'.) Secondly, can information technology fully ANTICIPATE all the future consequences of new discoveries and new systems it develops, upon the whole worlds environment, as well as mankind's intuition? (I say 'NO'.) I end this chapter with these two questions for you to determine your own answers.

Austerity: Its Causes, Culprits and Consequences

The first question (again) which we must address is what exactly is meant by 'austerity'? My dictionary includes a few definitions, but of particular significance to this book's subject and to us the people generally are the words 'harshness', 'severity', and 'inflexibility', being related to a nation's economic policy. (To my mind, the definition should also include 'dysfunctional national management!') Our nation's economic state directly and deeply concerns many aspects of the people's lives, wages, unemployment, increased cost of living, cuts in public services and so on. Looking back at the earlier definitions of 'democracy' given in Chapter 1, two elements seem to me to be particularly significant. Firstly 'active participation (in government rule) of the people' and secondly, 'channels of upward influence'. The 'harshness', 'severity', '(disgraceful) levels of prejudice', and 'inequality' of austerity decisions taken by a small elite government group and the banking institutions seem to me to satisfy two definitions of 'oligarchy' (the opposite of 'democracy') being 'public office protected by secrecy' (people being kept in the dark over a growing serious problem), and 'communication only downwards' (decisions taken by an elite group with the expectation of compliance by the people). We can therefore KNOW it is most of the people that suffer from 'austerity' and that the UK Government fails substantially on two basic standards of democracy.

To demonstrate this let us consider the real and now known circumstances of the 2007/20 period of UK austerity and recession. One of the main contributory factors was a banking crisis caused, it is said, by banks allowing far too much credit than was reasonable. Clearly the bank's 'elite' were more interested in interest generated income, more profits and higher payments to their 'investor' friends. Did not work though. Did it? This resulted in the government, in 2007 having to 'nationalise' the Northern Rock Bank, and in 2008, having to find £4 billion (?) rescue package for British banks. The year 2009 saw the UK – officially – in recession, followed by a record budget deficit of (wait for it!) £175 billion! Who, at the time, was blamed for this? The 'right wing' of the Conservative Party blamed the government 'overspending' by the previous Labour Party. The 'left' wing of the Labour Party blamed the banks' 'mismanagement'. The only reasonable conclusion to this is that the ensuing recession, which resulted in 'austerity' measures, was caused by both governments (Conservatives and Labour) AND greedy banking mismanagement, NOT us the people. Once again, we have a 'financial war', scenario and, like all kinds of 'war scenarios', it is us the people that suffer and, ultimately, must 'pick up the monetary tab' in various ways, rather than those who caused the problem. How was this done? By freezing public expenditure on services (health, education, police etc. etc.), freezing income inflationary rises, further restrictions on deserved social benefits, and even raising the retiring age! There are quite several references, articles and books/publications now demonstrating that the people LOST, the 'elite' WON. In an article in the *Times* newspaper (August 2022), again the consequences of bad governmental management by the government are well recorded, 'police give up on crime' and 'doctors having to leave the NHS'. At the same time banks and investors made fortunes, during 'austerity' measured in £Millions and in some cases £Billions, at the same time as wage restraint and redundancies were occurring amongst the people. Not convinced? To my mind a most impressive source of REAL, ACCURATE, information, is a BBC documentary series entitled 'The Decade the Rich Won'. It is, at the time of writing, available on 'BBC iplayer'. Do please watch it if you can. I assure you; you will become very angry! (Please dear 'non-voter', once again remember, YOU can make an enormous contribution to bring both the government and the 'Elite' to heel!)

I was personally affected by these series of events. I managed a large 'resources centre' for a Midlands local government council. The council, having been told of reduced government funds for public services, was forced to close various activities defined by ministerial directives. To the council's credit, they set up 'redeployment measures' to help employees who had been classified as 'at risk'. Vacancies arising in 'not at risk' services HAD to be first offered to suitable existing employees facing redundancy. (Proof thereby demonstrating that the further down you go through the various levels of governing organisations, the greater level of 'care' for people's livelihoods!) I, myself was transferred into another management position, to head a new personnel 'redeployment section' to carry out this task. During this time, my colleagues and I concluded that the government's 'austerity' policies were, in fact quite DAFT! How on earth, we concluded, could the 'national debt' be reduced by cutting the costs of important public services? Because the consequential increase in unemployment meant a large-scale reduction in government income (income tax, national insurance), AND reduced people's spending powers, which would help at least to restrict the growing national budget deficit. Our council, again to their credit, fully agreed with our opinions but had no alternative but to follow the government's directives. Additionally, it is not 'rocket science' nor 'naivety' to realise that the more money in the people's pockets/wallets, the more they can spend on services and goods, pay taxes, vat, council rates, etc.! They can BUY more, thereby increasing productivity and thus increasing employment followed by paying more income tax, that extends public funds! This is so simple and obvious which increases my suspicions of hidden, disgraceful levels of prejudice for the elite,

Now, with the benefit of hindsight, the truth is finally coming out. In (I think 2020?), the Institute of Public Policy Research (a registered professional, non-political 'think tank') defined 'austerity' as 'measures which depresses economic growth and, ultimately cause reduce tax revenues, that outweigh the "benefit" of reduced public spending'. The paper went on with 'Depressed economic growth, with austerity can increase... the "national debt"'. During the austerity period 2010/20, the UK economy 'shrank' by about £100 billion compared to what it would have been without the 'cuts'. (So, we 'workers' were right again!) But these consequences affect the economy even further because more unemployment, decreased wages, rising inflation, means people MUST spend less. Now in 2022 we find ourselves in the same scenario. The *Times* newspaper again gives out the consequences (August 2022). 'Police give up on crime', '£billions needed for effective sewage/ trade waste needed' etc. people no longer have the value of past income. Consequently 'sales' slump because of reduced 'buying power'. If sales slump, the commercial world suffers, resulting in even more 'economies' (unemployment) and wage restraints. And so it goes on. Again, with the benefit of hindsight we can now see who benefits from 'austerity'. More of this later.

I apologise for 'going on' so long about this aspect of prejudicial, mismanagement by the government and the commercial 'elite'. So, one last point on this subject. How specifically do we the population 'suffer' from austerity decisions made by the few? Firstly, increased unemployment. Please do not accept government statistics on this aspect. They are statistically and politically 'adapted' to suit political needs regularly. Then we have rising prices, cheaper environmentally dangerous products, wage raises for inflation severely restricted, and dangerous levels of reductions in public services. Of particular significance on this last item is the past statement by a police commissioner that 60% of all reported crimes are not dealt with. Then we have the regular incidents of emergency ambulances queueing at major UK hospitals to get attention for emergency case patients. A recent report from the county councils network estimates that county councils could face a £52 billion 'funding black hole' during the next six years (from 2019) resulting in more cuts to a variety of public services. Why do we get governments that cannot (will not?) accept the simpleness of truisms, that the higher the people's prosperity is, the higher the nation's economy is! Sorry, to keep on about this, but we MUST accept the reality of the consequences of bad management by the government. OK let's move on.

One often hears, in many levels of government activity, the expression 'taxation by stealth'. Again, at first, I dismissed this notion. Tax payments in whatever form is always recorded somehow, and I argued this point with my colleagues many years ago. Sometime later I bumped into my old colleague, and we chattered about old times. During our 'chat' I asked him what he meant by 'stealth taxation'. (His work used to be in relation to considering applications for social assistance from people suffering from various problems.) He explained why he used this expression. He said that three times, in a period of five years, new government 'guidelines' had been issued making it more difficult for applicants to meet the conditions required for obtaining government help/assistance for ill health, unemployment etc. Were these new conditions justified? I asked. 'No,' he said, only if you want to reduce the cost of public services by disguised means, which he strongly disagreed with, but had no choice but to refuse many more legitimate claims from people, clearly in need of help. Occasionally we see probable consequences of this kind of cost cutting. (March 2022). We read in a newspaper headline 'Biggest maternity scandal in history of the NHS'. This related to a catastrophic failure at 'Hospital Trusts' (private health services?) that may have led to the deaths of 201 babies in two decades. Someone really needs to investigate this! Let us have another 'Chilcote' style investigation which identifies that which our legal professions rightly define 'the truth, the whole truth, and NOTHING but the truth'.

So, if it is most of the people who suffer from austerity, did anyone benefit from government policies and the actions of banks and financial institutions, who effectively established the austerity situation? In a nutshell, it was the rich elite and specific regions of the UK who received the most benefit. This sounds dreadfully like an extreme 'socialist' talking, which I am certainly NOT. However, in Robert Preston's excellent book *WTF*, reference is made to an estimate by the Swiss investment bank 'Credit Suisse', that in 2013/14 (during one year of austerity in the UK), more 'dollar millionaires' were created in the UK than anywhere else in the world, except the USA! Even the Bank of England calculated that between 2006 and 2014, the change in 'net worth' of a typical person in the northeast of England and the Midlands was defined as 'negative'. In London, however it was 50% up! Moreover, a report in the 'i' newspaper (17/7/19, page 2), upon the 'wealthiest 'region in the UK, measured by 'medium family wealth per adult' (£000s) was the southeast (again!), scoring 176. This compared to 55 for the northeast of England, 83 for the west Midlands and 85 for the east Midlands. These kinds of facts justified much more publicity and attention than the media provided at that time.

A 'real-life' and typical example of this occurred more recently ('i' newspaper, March 2022) showing gross inequality and downright selfishness. I quote. 'The Boss of PO Ferries committed "Corporate Terrorism", by sacking 800 workers (with NO prior notice) and then replacing them with agency staff paid LESS than the official minimum wage' (!). This, at the same time as him continuing to receive £325,000 ANNUAL salary. He was (rightly in my view) labelled in the report as 'the most hated man in Britain'. My comment? Out of his salary and the increased company profits, should come full compensation for the 800 workers, I am sorry to HAVE to say this. Bring back workers' reasonable rights to strike! If you, dear reader have other (legal) ways of fighting this gross selfishness, do please let your MP know, reminding them about the date of the next general election. One other suggestion which comes to my mind is the reverse of the public coverage of 'best quality products'. Could we not, by applying proper criteria, name a product or service to be avoided by people, specifying why, e.g., environmental damage, unjust buying costs, unjust employment conditions, etc., managed by a people's jury, supported by independent professional people in appropriate disciplines?

There is, of course, a wide divergence of views amongst independent and knowledgeable economists upon the causes of austerity. Political parties always blame each other and/or use any other excuse they can think of. Whatever the truth is, one undeniable fact remains. Financial management and the economy of the nation is wholly vested in the 'elite' group of a few Parliament members, the UK Treasury, banking/ financial institutions, and the commercial world 'elite' (shareholders, company directors and CEOs). There is NO 'people'/'public' direct influence of any sort whatsoever. Consequently, the blame for economic mismanagement must lie solely with this group, and NOT 'the people' at large. Let us then put this assertion to the test of historically verifiable facts.

We have to go back some 40 years to discover the very beginnings of the economic crisis. Following the election of the Conservative government in 1979, the prime minister started a programme of 'deregulation and privatisation'. Initially, privatisation included independent bus companies and the railways. It also included reducing state regulation in essential commercialised infrastructure organisations (mainly banking and financial institutions). After the election of the Labour Party in 1997 the chancellor announced the 'freeing' of the Bank of England to set monetary policy. This freed the Bank of England from direct government control AND removed the power for controlling their financial activities (including overdrafts, and loans) by financial institutions. One other action by the government in 2006 ('Regulatory Reform Act 2006') empowered government ministers to make 'regulatory reform orders' to deal with older 'laws' that

THEY deemed to be irrelevant, obscure and out of date. This was criticised often, classifying it as 'the abolition of Parliament act', by delegating power to another portion of the 'elite' classes.

These Parliamentary acts by the two main political parties in power enabled banks to operate much more freely as a commercial financial institution in respect of credit, loans, interest rates, overdrafts and also 'monopolisation'. So far as privatisation of 'public services' was concerned, this brought in the wholly erroneous notion that the 'pursuit of profit' would improve services at less cost to public funds. Many criticisms have been expressed in the past by respected, well-informed professional financiers against these policies, but sadly fall on deaf ears. These expressed fears included risks of financial instability, reduced customer protection, inequality, dysfunctional management and unlimited risk-taking by banks and financial institutions. The actual results can now be clearly seen.

So, what happened next? A relatively small bank (no disrespect), the Royal Bank of Scotland, decided to adopt what I will describe as a vigorous 'monopolisation' policy and to buy control of many other banking/ financial institutions (including the much larger bank national Westminster), by raising, themselves additional capital. The 'equity' for this capital was the expected benefits of becoming more competitive, reducing the 'opposition' (other banks, etc.) and consequently greater profits. This policy was principally managed by an aggressive and ruthless chief executive officer. As well as managing these acquisitions, he applied extensive staff redundancies wherever he took control. Over an eight-year period he spent/committed funds which, in practical terms, the bank did not have, a fact which was clearly kept secret. The CEO became recognised and famous and was (would you believe this!) 'knighted' for his work. (He has since been 'de knighted'!) The earlier warnings of professional independent financiers, in a few hours, suddenly became realism. Shareholders on the stock market suddenly realised that this 'monopolisation' had gone far enough because RBS was going to run out of cash. The chairman ('CEO') of RBS made an urgent call to the government chancellor asking for urgent government help. If this was not forthcoming immediately, RBS would crash into bankruptcy resulting in a 'knock on' effect on the whole UK stock/banking market. After finding out what amount of public funding support was needed ('£billions'), the chancellor asked, what now can be recorded as an infamous historical question, with an equally infamous answer: 'How long can you last?' Was the question. The answer (would you believe!) was 'HOURS'. If some authoritative statement of government support was not issued before share trading on the stock market commenced at 8 am. the following day, the UK would be effectively become 'broke' because of the 'knock on' effect throughout the

UK shares market. The government HAD to step in, again – by increasing the national debt. We have had a succession of these major corporations failing and then expecting public funds from the government to bail them out. The latest attempt (currently) is the airline holiday organisation Thomas Cook going bust and asking the government to use public funds to bail them out. If they refuse, how many more people will go into unemployment needing benefits from the government. This has got to stop! The total national debt must now be measured in £trillions that the present generation of people will be paying for, their children will be paying for, and probably their grandchildren as well. This is a fact. Does this not worry you? I have not caused this situation. YOU have not caused this situation! Extreme capitalistic policies are the major cause. The BBC Two channel broadcasted a most important documentary on this subject in July 2019 entitled 'The Bank That Almost Broke Britain'. Well worth looking at! (If it is still available)

This 'national debt' scenario worries me deeply. In an article by 'Wikipedia' (July 2020), a simple graph is displayed showing the 'UK debt as a percentage of GDP (1993–2018)'. This showed that the lowest national debt in this particular period was in 2001 at 26%. The highest was in 2018 at 86%!

Are we, the people, still being exploited by this unregulated, dreadful level and type of government mismanagement? It is my perspective we still are, in many ways. Try a simple test for yourself. Put the TV on (commercial channels) and for once watch the adverts (I know, a 'pain in the arse' job!) but watch for those advertisements offering loans. Ignore the stuff about new cars, luxury cruises and so on, look at the (very) small print at the bottom of the screen. Look quick because it is not shown throughout the advert! You will see a % figure called the 'APR'. This tells you, without going into the details and conditions, how much interest you will be charged in one year for whatever money you borrow. I have seen figures quoted of 40%, 60% and in one case, 99%! Then please do the maths, before even picking up the phone. To my mind this unregulated pressure on people who, through no fault of their own, are struggling to make ends meet, is happening because the financial markets are exploiting the vulnerable in order to help them survive the situation which they themselves have helped to create.

One final reference to the government's past performance and the past actions of banks in directing the nation's economy is provided by another excellent study paper published in September 2013 by Oxfam. The title of the paper is 'The true cost of austerity and inequality' (in the UK). Even though this paper does not, of course, relate to the recent six/seven years or so, the paper provides verifiable facts about the UK's economy during the period preceding 2013. Amongst other (very important) matters, the paper tells us the following. 'The socio-economic reforms of the 1980s involved a shift towards market-based capitalism, characterised by financial liberalisation, the erosion of social security and deregulation of the labour market (employment). These reforms have led to a dramatic increase in the number of people living in poverty, which almost doubled from 7.3 million in 1979 to 13.5 million in 2008, driven by the growing share of income going to the richest. In particular, the top one percent. The UK now ranks as one of the most unequal countries in the OECD. The 2008 financial crisis led to the UK Government having to "bail out" British banks at an estimated cost of £141 billion, with exposure to liabilities of over £1 trillion.' The article goes on.

'Since 2010, austerity – primarily, in the form of deep spending cuts in public service, with comparatively small increases in tax, has been the UK's dominant fiscal policy, with fewer measures to stimulate the economy. Whilst austerity measures have had some impact in reducing the deficit, they have delivered little growth and the public debt has risen from 56.6% of gross domestic product in 2009 to 90% in 2014 (£1.39 trillion).'

So, let us now come back in time to the present day (2022). Yet again we are, in reality, in RECESSION. Some of this is due to the Russian/Ukraine War and the economic battles between nations. Petrol prices rocketing, cost of living items going up, incomes reducing and, once again, public services cutbacks. To quote a report in the 'i' newspaper (28/3/22), 'The NHS is in danger of losing thousands of vital medical staffing because of stiff competition from workers from (you have guessed it!) high street firms (private medical organisations). Supermarkets, coffee shops and logistic firms are among those promoting wages higher than the lowest hourly rate in the public sector'. So, our public funded NHS provides less and less public health services for 'the poor', the wealthier can afford to go 'private' in health care, more profits for the 'business elite'. My appraisal? 'The struggles for power between extreme capitalism and extreme socialism is the ROOT cause.' Next consequence on the national debt? I just do not want to go there!

These vitally important points are just a sample of many others of great concern and hidden from the view of the people. So, let me now replace my 'citizen's cap' and offer my comments, in that role.

- Considering the staggering monetary figures quoted above, is it not a painfully obvious case of total government and financial institutional incompetence, greed and mismanagement? Surely, the causes and the culprits have to be identified, whether they are government ministers, senior government officers, the leaders of banks and major commercial organisations. My opinion? Those that caused it should be forcefully charged for it! (YES. Super tax and profits limitations!) Why not?)

- If the foregoing presumption is justified (I do not see how it cannot be), should not we the people be now demanding an extensive, independent, non-political official 'Chicote' style public inquiry, comprising a combination of professional economists, independent financiers, high court judges and a large 'citizens panel'? (Readers may recall that a past public inquiry, chaired by Sir John Chilcote, and charged with the task of reviewing the circumstances of the Iraq War. This resulted in identifying an appalling level of criticisms of ministerial failings, bad government decisions and falsehoods.)

- We are persuaded, are we not, that the rule of law is applicable to everyone, regardless of rank, status, position etc. If a comprehensive 'Chicote' style of Inquiry DID identify serious levels of prejudice, mismanagement, abuse of power, false representation, upon vitally important economic circumstances, and no disclosure of nationally important economic/ financial factors, should not those responsible be identified AND considered for criminal charges under the Fraud Act 2006 (false representation, failure to disclose information, abuse of position?) I really would like to hear a barrister's opinion on this. If this is not possible under existing laws, new laws need to be introduced.

- If those identified by a proper professional and public inquiry as being responsible for this ongoing crisis (considering the colossal amounts of public money involved) are NOT brought to account, then the law is NOT equal to everyone. If this was the case, the only way to satisfy the rule of 'law equality', would be to release all the prisoners serving prison sentences for considerably less amounts of 'fraudulently' obtaining money and pay them compensation, as has happened in the more recent RBS CEO case!

There must be a professional, independent, comprehensive and open public inquiry of the past 20 years of the government's and the banks' mismanagement of the nation's economic position. And considering the excessive amount of time it took the Chilcote Inquiry to publish its report (caused by various refusals to provide relevant, accurate information), such an inquiry should have the right, enshrined by statute, to have full access to all relevant public documents. If the courts continue to send people to prison under the fraud acts for fraud involving thousands of pounds, should we not send MPs, bank CEOs and 'others' to prison for losing £billions of pounds of OUR money? Again, I thought our laws were applied to everyone.

My perspective? The UK, through government policies, political deceit and commercial greed, has now become an undemocratic debt dependant nation. Very profitable for the elite/minority, but appalling inequality for the majority. How can we, powerless as we may be at present, influence change, for our own futures? The voice of the people in the Brexit referendum result was most unpopular to the politicians, the government, banks, sections of the media and commerce. The consequence, being three years of futile negotiations, time wasting (at enormous cost to public funds), in the hope that somehow, the referendum result could be overturned or 'safely', ignored. There are ways for us, the people, to change things. Voting at elections is only one way.

But for the moment let us concentrate on our own expenditure habits in ways that will make our own financial positions better AND exercise more control over the actions of the 'elite' classes. We do have one particularly important weapon. Our wallets and purses. By reducing our borrowings, mortgages, overdrafts and all other forms of debt, individually, the cumulative result of thousands of us doing the same thing will be given much more notice than elections or referendums. Easier said than done? True, not many of us can pay off debts, mortgages, loans etc. at a stroke. But what many of us can do is to make greater effort to REDUCE, rather than INCREASE our debts and expenditure. Mortgage payments can be increased voluntarily, with surprising reductions in the annual interest charges. Try to ignore the flagrant harassment by financial sections to take on even more debt. Reduce your outgoings by cutting out unnecessary expenditure. On gas, electricity, telephone, TV, insurance charges, shop around for cheaper deals. You will ALWAYS find savings and whilst your own individual changes will have little impact on the wider economic picture, if thousands of people started doing this, much more notice will be given than that given towards election/referendum results.

One other point comes to mind relating to austerity and the democratic principal of transparency, particularly at general election times, is this. Should not the retiring governmental party be required to publish an audited statement of clearly specified and relevant economic changes and national expenditure and income, as is required for 'lower' sections of government levels (county councils, district councils, education, health, public safety, etc.), but fully audited by professional, independent auditors for the period of their tenure of office, as well as their original political manifesto? Do we, the ratepayers and taxpayers not have a right to have access to such wholly verifiable facts published by a professional, non-political body? If we the people do not start by insisting upon these kinds of actions (and other ways) to bring the 'elite' sections more under our control, we are simply piling up more trouble times for our future offspring generations. This must start with reducing the obnoxious levels of secrecy, inequality and unregulated capitalism. (And I repeat, by avoiding turning to extreme *socialism* as an alternative to extreme *capitalism*.)

I will end this long (and painful!) chapter upon austerity on an important question for you to consider. The question is 'who ACTUALLY creates the nation's wealth in the UK?' I have several answers to that question but my own 'ten' best people (of course, there will be more), are as follows. You dear reader, may well have more.

- The teachers in schools, colleges and universities. Who educate and pass on knowledge and training, thereby enabling and empowering ALL people to make a positive contribution to the nation's development in their working lives.
- The factory workers who produce all the products needed both within the nation, and abroad.
- Public sector workers (health, police, administration, etc., etc.).
- The armed forces who defend our nation.
- The farmers and agriculturists who feed the nation and protect the environment.
- The construction/building trades workers who meet the many needs in society as a whole.
- The professional workers (scientists, lawyers, marketing and sales, architects, etc., etc.)
- The voluntary sector, who try to fill the gaps in people's needs.
- The artists, actors, singers, etc. who entertain, and enrich people's lives.

- Transport, roads, railways, sea cargo, airlines.
- Communications information technology etc.

Beyond all other factors relating to the prosperity of a nation, these and others are the real 'WEALTH GENERATORS', and yet they are the last to benefit from their work, compared to the 'elite' classes. Their voices MUST be heard AND accommodated, in any truly democratic nation.

The Hidden Enemies of Democracy

My opening question on this chapter is why the whole world is virtually in such a growing 'mess', economically, inequality, wars (actual or threatened), declining environment, injustice, poverty, famine and many other factors. The answer to my mind is so simple, and surprisingly not realised by most of the world's populations. We have an increasing level of 'bad' leaders of nations. Be they political, religious, billionaires, military, banks, and other kinds of 'the elite'. The overwhelming vast majority of the peoples of all nations do not want wars, economic battles, religious conflicts, deceits, 'inconvenient truths', unrestrained 'power holders', dreadful levels of inequality and criminal leaders. It is this growing level of selfishness of bad leaderships, which is the major factor of the world's troubles. Hence, the title of this book, written by an 'ordinary bloke' in an average nation, which, no doubt, will be condemned by all those with vested and selfish interests and ambitions. Put simply, they do NOT want real DEMOCRACY. Their endless fight is for nothing less than more personal POWER, and personal wealth.

In other chapters, I have briefly described the circumstances of the more obvious elements of 'anti-democracy' (information technology, representativeness of the UK's electoral system, dictatorships, ignoring and/or distorting democracy principals, etc.). Sadly, there are many more cases which adversely affect democracy and the wishes and needs of a nation's people. These situations are even more serious because, understandably, ordinary citizens (like me) do not normally realise their presence, and more importantly, what their impact is, upon the nation's level of democracy, and people's basic rights. So how do we translate out suspicions into fully justified, knowledgeable and accurate opinions? By researching beyond the propaganda dished out by the 'elite', from more authoritative independent non-political sources. Once again, I am greatly indebted for the writings, reports and research findings of many distinguished, authoritative, articles and the writings of knowledgeable authors and professional, independent institutions. Their collective warning should NOT be ignored! I have found so much provable evidence of growing 'oligarchy', extreme and growing capitalism and socialism in politics, constant attempts at world domination by various large nations, religious dictatorships, abuse of information technology, uncontrolled commercialism, unjust restrictions upon people's fundamental rights and

'SOCIAL irresponsibility'. These are the situations which in my view fully justify the use of the word CRISIS in this book's title.

There are clear signs that 'ordinary people' like myself, worldwide, have the same suspicions that I had originally, but could only wish and hope for a better world. In my first book, *The Opportunity of Unemployment*, I referred to a past hit song entitled 'You gotta seek the hero inside yourself', sung by 'M people'. A beautiful piece of music which gave an important message to people, particularly those suffering from the experience of unemployment (being just one aspect of governmental mismanagement). The message from this piece of music was we all have natural abilities, strengths and talents. Identify and understand these, then use them! My music selection for this book and in particular this chapter sung by (amongst others) Harry Secombe and Tony Bennet is 'If I ruled the world'. Another wonderful piece of music created by gifted people who wanted to convey an important message as 'ordinary people'. Within the lyrics are the words 'every voice would be a voice to be heard' and 'every man (person) would see the world as his friend', and finally 'there would be happiness that no man (person) could end', to quote just three wishes of the song. Other wishes in this song could be viewed as 'impossible dreams', but the essential point here is the acknowledgement that people do believe things are seriously wrong and do honestly wish for a better world.

As said already, I join this universal hope as an ordinary citizen, that ALL people will rise and force change by effective actions which are none violent and within the law. It really is possible to do this by carefully coordinated action and careful planning.

'Every voice would be a voice to be heard'. The 'elite' would have us believe this is impossible to achieve. Not so now! The colossal development of worldwide information technology, which we have seen from an earlier chapter in this book, is progressively being used abusively for the principal of acquiring, retaining, and extending power just for the various 'elite' classes throughout the world. BUT 'IT' can be a two-edged sword. It can be used to reverse this trend to bring back real power BACK to the people. This is not a big deal. Amongst us, the people, are our own 'IT' whizz-kids, quite capable of creating a people's own 'Silicon Valley'.

Both history and the world today clearly demonstrate that these 'elitist' extremes literally destroy democracy. Wars, people persecutions, terrorism, despicable acts of cruelty and injustice would fill a whole library of records. Whole nations have had to be divided, just to limit such atrocities. Conversely, whole nations are 'taken over' by larger nations as we shall see in later chapters.

I have a memory of something my very dear mother told me when I was a teenager, and we were talking about some war or another. My mother, related to me the day that her farther, my dear grandad, returned home from the First World War trenches. (Grandad was a sergeant in a Nottinghamshire regiment.) When my mother, sisters and brothers, as children, recognised him walking home, down the street, they rushed to greet him, arms open wide, 'It's Dad,' they shouted. He said, straight away to Grandma, 'Keep them away, my love, from me. Now, I am lousy (infected with lice) and need a good hot bath first.' Afterwards, with my grandmother holding him and with his children on his knee all weeping with relief and happiness, he said to my dear Grandma, with tears in his eyes, 'I don't know what the world is coming to, love.' He had seen so many atrocities and awful scenes, but he had survived, and was back safe, with his beloved family. So many people had suffered so much more. That's the reason Grandad's words are a lifelong and important memory to me. They sum up the way people are being denied the truth ('I don't know') and their serious concern for the future. (Actual future event? Second World War ending with the first use of nuclear weapons!) His words are the words of SO many ordinary people in the whole world. A simple example, yet again, of the 'collective wisdom of the people' being sadly ignored. Another terrible war, caused only by the 'elite' levels in nations' governments, simply hell bent (!) on their own 'personal power' characteristics! This simple, heartfelt question from Grandad, sums up in one person's words the whole theme/purpose of this book. What actually is wrong and how might this be changed for the future benefit of the human race and this beautiful world of ours, i.e., 'what the world SHOULD be coming to'.

Coming back to the present day, what is happening now (2022)? Russia is starting a war with another much smaller nation. Other large nations are making threatening noises if Russia does this. My message to the Russian people is this. Refuse to go to war! Otherwise THE WORLD WILL HAVE THE THIRD WORLD WAR! Using even more dreadful weapons of mass destruction that, ONCE AGAIN, we do not even know about! What was it, again, that my dear grandad once said? I would also remind the people of Russia, that their grandparents fought and died in a revolution to eliminate the royal family elite and bring in real socialism, with power coming back to the people. Now they suffer from another elite dictatorship under extreme socialism.

So, how can we 'ordinary' people today recognise that our democracy is again being threatened to the point that a disaster of one type or another is imminent? We take less notice of some of the sections of the media, and what 'political' propaganda is being issued, and take more notice of the responsible media and more notice of non-political, independent, professional researchers and institutes, before considering our own opinions. THEN consider what we can do (legally) ourselves, to bring our leaders 'to heel'!

I will quote just two examples of the words of just two independent, authoritative authors. Firstly, Julian Linz gave us four warning signs of 'authoritarian' (dictatorship). They were:

- Rejection of the generally accepted rules of democratic competition, i.e., a leader who refuses to accept the results of an election (or a referendum).
- Refuses to accept the legitimacy of democratic opponents.
- Endorses, ignores or encourage violence.
- Expresses augments supporting crackdowns on civil liberties, i.e., controlling laws, financial, legal, action against opponents, workers' rights.

Then we have an even more worrying 'enemy' of democracy, given to us in an excellent book *How Democracies Die* by Steven Levitsky and Daniel Ziblatt. To quote. 'One of the greatest ironies of how democracies die is that the very defence of democracy is often use as a pretext for its subversion (!). Would-be autocrats often use economic crises, natural disasters and (perceived) security threats (wars, alliances – UKRAINE!), insurgencies, 'terrorism', to justify what is, in reality, anti-democracy measures'. How very, very true!

With the benefit of information technology (yes 'IT' CAN be and is a good thing!) we can access many more sources of 'good' information and data to enable us to recognise the warning signs and early symptoms of 'democracy under siege'. I will refer to yet another such source. (There are quite a few.) A most commendable paper issued by an American author, Dambisa Moyo in 2018. Here, the author specifies, for us, 'ten (further) warning signs' that democracy is becoming threatened, without us, the people, releasing it. I quote (and recommend) this most helpful criteria.

- Voter participation is weak and even failing. (Recall in an earlier chapter we showed that currently about one third of the total number of eligible voters did NOT vote in the most recent UK general election.)
- Money buying political power. (Influencing the media, contributions to political parties, 'Commercial' influence in national policies.)
- Key pillars of 'liberal democracy' are weakening. (In the USA, the US 'executive' (presidential levels), legislature, and the judiciary.) National leaders are making more and more decisions circumventing the legislative processes, even to the extent of waging wars, i.e., political dysfunction, judicial inequality.
- The average tenures of elected leaders are falling, over time. A sign of internal political battles for individual power. (On this particular note, it was an ironic coincidence that at the same time as typing this very relevant 'sign', I read the morning's

'i' newspaper – 22/1/22. Within separate pages, there were no less than three individual reports referring to incidents where three of the worldwide most powerful national leaders' 'popularity ratings' were on the decline. Proof positive? Now (2023) in the UK, I bring it.)

- Democracies being increasingly challenged from 'within' by social media. (Unjust headlines, 'cartoon' characteristics, sensationalism etc.)
- Political 'freedom' is declining.
- Trust in political structures is waning. (In the USA only about 18% trust the government in Washington. It was about 60% in the 1960s.)
- Non-democratic nations are gaining favour (over other more democratic nations).
- We have created 'illiberal' democracies. (About 70% of the world, deemed 'democratic', are not democratic at all!)
- The younger generation are turning away from 'democracy'. (Statistical evidence to support this view is becoming increasingly available.)
- Political prejudice and inequality. In an impressive front-page article in the *Guardian* (May 2023), relating to the government's 'honours lists' ('peerage' awards), the outrageous level of extraordinary and unjustified prejudice in nominating 'personal allies and own family' for national awards and 'peerage' (House of Lords membership) was clearly shown

(e.g., a former prime minister's father?!). My personal view? Let's reverse the prejudice aspect in favour of the nation's people who have given their lives and souls to achieve real benefit for the nation's people (scientists, health workers, police heroes, lifetime teachers, academics, engineers, etc.). NO politicians at all! They have already been well rewarded for doing little already! 'LEVELLING UP?' in reality? Bring it on!

Regarding the first 'sign', quoting again from Niheer Diandi's excellent book *In Favour of the Nation's Democracy Failing*, he rightly states, 'the biggest challenge facing democracy today is widespread citizen's indifference and disengagement'. How very true. Democracy cannot survive if more and more lose interest in public matters, elections, referendums and government actions. 'Use it, or lose it' is an expression I will use repeatedly. Democracy has not failed yet, but it is like cancer. We only suspect things are not right, but we put it out of our minds, until it becomes too late (recall Russian history). Like cancer, we need to deal with it now to stand any chance of restoring proper and just standards of democracy.

In respect of Dambisa's second 'sign' above, I accept that such organisations are, indirectly, contributing towards one principal of democracy in respect of 'representative bodies' (political parties) as specified in the basic criteria for democracy. (Those bodies can only function with some financial resources.) Nonetheless there MUST be more control, decreed by statute, clearly identifying and prohibiting clear signs of buying favour from an incoming government. My personal view is that it would not be a considerable strain if the political groups, after an election, are given capital grants from public funds proportionate to the number of votes given by the electorate to the party. If we can find public money to pay the 'peers' in the House of Lords for doing little (or nothing) some of that money could be transferred to the House of Commons parties in accordance with the voters' choices at the election. Any other 'donations' would then be much more controlled and monitored. Nevertheless, the ten principals defined above gives us, the people, even more justification for demanding democracy restoration.

Distracting the public attention. It is becoming increasingly obvious now to us all that governments are using what has been previously described as 'engineering the views of the nation's people'. To use a simple example to illustrate this point, during the current crisis of the coronavirus pandemic, government statements and most of the news media concentrated our (the people's) attention upon the certain circumstances of this crisis. What we are getting is propaganda from the government about what 'they' are doing to combat this most serious problem by telling us all what the experts are advising.

Again, in other words, appearing to be doing something, when effectively doing nothing themselves. All this does is feed the media with opportunities for more 'competing sensationalism'. The real heroes who are fighting this dreadful situation are the medics in hospitals, the scientists who are working flat out to perfect treatments for the coronavirus pandemic, the people who offer their bodies to test effectiveness of vaccines and US, the people wearing face masks and applying 'distancing' measure to limit passing on infections. Do we hear of the thousands of jobs being lost, the hundreds of businesses closing, and the financial consequences upon the nation's economy. Sorry, no, 'not good PR'. We have a right to know these things and what the government can do, and equally important, what it cannot do in these cases. When this pandemic is finally beaten, the next crisis will be austerity (yet again!?). So, is this not yet another example of distraction tactics from other more important information for reasons solely to do with retention of power?

Finally on this subject may I express the view that we owe it to the millions of people, worldwide, who have sadly died from the disease and their loved ones, that the true original cause of coronavirus is identified by professional experts in appropriate disciplines and that any nation who obstructs this work should be condemned by all other nations of our world? (Including those who falsely claim acknowledgements for positive actions, given by others.)

World's Population Explosion

According to web information, the current world population is estimated to increase by about 8 million per year for the foreseeable future. According to the United Nations figures, most of the world's population growth is in 'poor' countries. The 47 'least developed' countries are expected to see their collective population nearly double from roughly 1 billion to 1.9 billion by 2050. The two nations which have by far the largest population in the world are China at 1,442,475,406 followed by India at 1,387,770,155. Third place is the USA at 332,106,729. Fourth place is Indonesia at 275,181,062 and fifth place is Pakistan at 223,384,802. (The UK is outside the top 20 and is not even listed).

It is therefore not too difficult to see that this rate of population growth decreases the overall world's sustainability and democracy levels, and this is not even the worst danger to our planet. The world simply cannot continue to support this uncontrolled growth of the human population. Sadly, yet realistically, the only controlling events to population growth are famines, wars and diseases. To my mind, there has been only one attempt at containment of population growth, which occurred in China, who, some years ago, tried to introduce a 'family size limit' of only two children. The current coronavirus – allegedly started in Wuhan, China – is the current incident of 'ppulation' control (what a dreadful way of describing this!). Does this vitally important factor ever get the attention of the world's governing bodies, or the world's media. NO! (Not good PR.) We now hear that China's 'family size' policy is being replaced. I wonder what the real reason is for this change of mind.

This population explosion is much more serious for 'island' nations like our own. The population of just England and Wales has reached a historical high of 59,597,300 according to the first results from a 2021 census. The count was based upon questionnaires filled out by households on the 21st March 2021 and is a 6.3% increase on the 2011 figure of 56,075,912. England now ranks as the second most densely populated country in Europe, after Netherlands, based upon figures from Eurostat. England's land size is 130,279km. We would need our land size to grow by another nearly 8,000km just to maintain the same ratio of population to land size! (More detailed statistics in the next chapter)

I do not believe that the world's 'elite' does not want you to realise this. The 'capitalist' elite' will only see more people, more sales/trading, more profits and more dividends to shareholders. Governments will see greater populations, more public money, more bureaucracy, more MPs. The religious 'elite' will see more converts to their own religions. I confess, I do not have a clue upon the best remedy. It is a problem that must be faced up to. (Improving real democracy in the poorer countries with safer lifestyles might help.) This is, seriously a CRISIS, which needs to be addressed humanely, somehow.

The global environmental CRISIS

At first glance, you could rightly ask 'what has the environmental crisis got to do with democracy decline?' (We saw earlier that 'social responsibility' standards were not, in the least, being considered from that angle). Initially, I held the same view about the relationship with democracy decline. However, it maybe worth checking out this reaction. So back to the web. What, precisely is creating this very serious problem? i.e., CAUSES of global environmental change/warming. Up comes a very clear response.

Six causes of GLOBAL warming

1. Oil and gas.
2. Deforestation/industrial activities.
3. Waste (from people)/agricultural livestock.
4. Power plants affecting the atmosphere.
5. Exhaust emissions, vehicles, trains, aircraft.

6. Consumerism. E.g., plastics, refuse, other 'non-recyclable' materials.

To this list, we may add other living species being wiped out, and last, but by no means least, mankind's growing population size.

OK, so, a big and very serious problem, rightly defined as a worldwide CRISIS. How, then, is democratic decline (which is, essentially a human being/mankind matter) involved? Looking at the recognised and clear causes, the 'culprits' are blatantly clear, to me, at least. Every single item above is caused by one 'life form' only, human beings, no one else. Second question is the '50 dollar' question. 'Who leads the people?' Answer. Unrestrained governments, unrestrained commercialism, unrestrained capitalism and socialism) with the scientific community providing knowledge, without appreciating the full consequences of their 'discoveries'. Not benefiting the 'rank and file' of the human population. Did you or I know when the first use of 'plastics' was introduced, what the effect it would have on the world oceans? There is the connection to democracy decline, the world's 'elite', who are obsessed with gaining more and more power and personal wealth and thereby ruining our beautiful world, by their decisions and actions. A full justification, to my mind, for classifying democracy decline, as a real WORLDWIDE CRISIS of equal (if not higher) level importance to the environmental CRISIS.

Is there an example of the above, where the people, and the world, could benefit from a development, that the 'elite' are not interested in (for 'power and profit') considerations? I believe there is. One aspect of the listing above totally ignores a tremendous worldwide source of power (electric kind) which has absolutely no detrimental effect on the planet's environment whatsoever. It does not use physical materials (coal, gas, oil, minerals) all of which create monetary profits plus considerable environmental damage. This other resource is FREE and has no damaging effect on the environment at all. And it is CLEAN. This most powerful resource is simply WATER.

The whole planet is covered two thirds by water in oceans and seas, permanently in a state of tidal movement. This is not all. Lakes, rivers streams, waterfalls are also widely prevalent. The essential aspect of this is WATER MOVEMENT, every second, day and night, without pause. Tidal movement, flowing rivers, waterfalls permanently in a state of movement. Solar energy is good from day and sun light, but not at night. Wind power is good when the wind blows. Water movement is permanent, the world over. Why are we not using this for generating electricity worldwide in all cases where there is movement? From immense TIDAL power, worldwide, right down to rivers and streams, lakes, even domestic rainwater drainage systems. So, come on you scientist/engineers! Give us a wide variety of simple, cheap different systems of generating free power from all forms of water movement, which has NO detriment upon any aspect of the living environment and water animal/ plant live forms. Another remedy which thankfully is now being recognised is 'solar farms'. Problem is once these options are brought into operation, not much opportunity for profit or power acquisition. Shame!

Religious diversity worldwide

In attempting to identify the hidden 'enemies' of democracy, it would be manifestly unjust not to discuss the world's religions in this context, without firstly unreservedly acknowledging and applauding the immeasurable number of benefits to the whole human race given by all the main religions of the world. As a UK Christian I have been given high quality medical treatment by a Muslim doctor. I have listened to most impressive lectures from Hindu lecturers and even had training, playing football from a Jewish sports trainer. My own religion is endlessly raising supportive funding for disadvantaged people throughout the whole world. Long may these wonderful endeavours continue. (Also, it is not often realised that most of all major religions have so much in common in relation to their beliefs, protocols, historical events, laws and wisdom.)

But, in this imperfect world of ours, all situations have some level of human imperfections and 'negativity'. So, first some facts about world religions taken from

'Wikipedia'. Religious populations listed proportionately total some 12 main groups worldwide. The highest proportion worldwide in percentage terms is Christianity at 31% followed by Islam at 24%, Hinduism at 15% and 'unaffiliated' at about 15%, and Buddhism at about 6%. All these religions have their own version of 'God' and the rules and principals for mankind. As with the whole subject of 'democracy', the rules can be interpreted by various factions within each religion in different ways. Again, as with democracy, different religious leaders are acknowledged and their writings recorded in many religious transcripts, Bibles, and are often engraved in stone at religious sites throughout the world.

Almost certainly, all these different approaches give rise to disputes between various religious doctrines. Result? History clearly shows many nations resort to wars, both nationally and internally giving rise to more disputes and separations within nations, based entirely on religious grounds. The whole world's history is littered with so many of these wars with appalling consequences of brutality, mass killings, torture and dictatorships. The 'Middle East' seems to be a permanent area of war scenarios, the Irish nation is divided by two branches of Christianity (Protestant/Catholic), the whole Indian f had to be divided into two separate nations (India and Pakistan). The fact is therefore that the rights of people to freely choose their own beliefs and religions is progressively denied.

If there is so much in common between religion principles and concepts, why cannot all religions in the world come together and create a universal declaration of people's rights to choose their own religions freely and without restraint? In the meantime, I am afraid it is an unavoidable conclusion that despite the overwhelming beneficial contributions to humans, religion at this time IS contrary to the basic principles of democracy. I will emphasise this point further. We have the benefit of various protocols for defining both democracy/oligarchy, social responsibility, the ten commandments, definition of crime, etc. etc. Is it not time for ALL the religions of the world to develop and adopt their own worldwide declaration of religious protocols to set a new standard of mutual respect/rights/behaviour, for ALL religions and beliefs in the world? Again, religious 'elites' would strongly oppose this, of course. So, such an action could only be developed by the religious congregations themselves, resisting the 'wrath' of 'elite leaders.' Many of whom, it has to be said, are only interested in advancing their own power and influence in the world.

Not convinced? Consider the following news reports from responsible news media sources. Easter terrorism/ killings in Sri Lanka. Death toll soars to 290, and about 500 more injured. The deadliest violence since the end of the civil war in 2009. Attacks comprise of bombing during Easter services at Christian churches in Negombo, Batticaloa and Colombo and three tourists' hotels in the country's capital. 'Suicide bombers' were used at some of the sites. Attackers are thought to be a 'radical extremist Islamist group'. In 2018, a state of emergency was declared after members of the Buddhist Sinhala community attacked mosques and Muslim-owned properties. The world's largest religious group, Christianity, has a long history of attacks against other religions, notable in the Middle East, but also in the Far East (India) and Africa. The 'Twin Towers' (America) might be viewed as the very worst example of religious killings of innocent people of different religious persuasions. As with all other kinds of wars, designed, encouraged and managed by a (religious) ELITE, This must cease!

Information technology

We considered the growing dangers of information technology in an earlier chapter. However, another excellent book has been published on the subject of 'Hidden dangers to democracy', by Jamie Bartlett, who is regarded as 'one of the world's leading experts on the digital revolution' ('The people vs tech'). Jamie describes how information technology is reducing democracy, by 'engineering' people's views and 'prioritising' (election) manifestos promises, which can then be 'dumped' by carefully selected facts, in order – simply – to maintain personal power (in government). I am, personally, quite ignorant upon the intricacies of 'IT', but Jamie's book (interpreted into my 'IT dummy' level!) means to me that ANY and ALL information about us the people from literally billions of different sources, can be (by highly complex software) interpreted into what we the people like to hear, with the sole objective of obtaining, retaining and increasing individual power. The problem is that ordinary citizens (like me), cannot understand the complexities of this growing trend, and even worse, are limited in what action we can take to deal with this most dangerous situation. My only hope is that independent IT professionals who have a strong desire to maintain and improve democracy, will follow Jamie's lead, and perhaps create a worldwide convention which specifically bans (by legal statute) aspects of this growing danger in a way which is clear and easy to understand. Then we the people can bring our pressure to help control this growing threat.

The growth of political divisions and national identities in the UK

Yet another well researched information publication entitled 'The electoral divisions of the United Kingdom' by Awan Scully argues that since 1950, successive elections have demonstrated a growing level of separation on 'internal nations grounds, with the influence of new political parties specifically concerned with countries'.

The SNP for Scotland openly calling for independence. Plaid Cymru for the Welsh nation, and in Northern Ireland, both the DUP and Sinn Feign parties. But this 'dividing factor' goes even further. It is the (in my view) ridiculously large number of separate 'political' parties who stood for election in the most recent UK 2019 general election. Outside the three 'largest' parties (Conservative, Labour and Liberal), and the four 'nationalist' parties, over 60 small 'local' or 'special interest' parties are listed in the HM government library website 2019 general election. Total votes and seats for each 'party' are minimal, producing no 'seats' in the government. (Talk about 'divide and conquer', if we ever get invaded, we have already done this for our enemy!) Also, all this does is to openly demonstrate the undeniable fact that the government elected always comes from one of the two 'extremes', Conservative or Labour, with a significant majority of voters opposed to the incoming government. This, without considering the growing number of 'non-voters'. How can this whole situation identify 'the collective will of the people?'

The reality of representational principles in the UK

All MPs in the UK Parliament are required to act within an openly published 'code of conduct'. Section 3 of the code states 'members shall have a duty to act in the interests of the nation, as a whole, and a special duty to their constituents'. Can we really presume at the present time that 'self-interests' (e.g., above all else remaining as an MP, improving their Parliamentary status, earning 'second' incomes, etc.) NEVER enters their mind before the interests of either 'the nation as a whole' or the 'wishes of their constituents' as they CHOOSE to see it? And can we not also assume that party loyalty, even when wrong action or unequal policies are contemplated, 'representativeness' still get priority? If these presumptions are correct then is this why the public have a growing distrust in MPs and politics generally, as shown in current, responsible, social research studies?

In relation further to the 'representativeness' aspect of democracy, it is interesting to note that in the 'lower' levels of the UK's government structures (county councils, borough councils, town and parish councils), the representativeness requirement becomes much more direct than is the case for Parliamentary MPs. I quote from a local borough council's website. This states 'that a councillor's role is to champion the needs of residents, the whole community and, in a special way ALL constituents, including those who did not vote for me, putting their interests first'. Further evidence that the further up the political ladder you travel, the less they care about the wishes of the electorate. (Perhaps, one day, local councils may tell the government how to act, rather than the other way round!)

The final 'enemy' of democracy

The final 'culprit' in this chapter on 'Enemies of Democracy' is not going to be popular amongst a rising proportion of the UK's population. But it MUST be accepted. The person is none other than the 'Non-VOTER'. To my mind, the most important element in any democracy is the unrestrained right of people to freely vote in the election of the nation's governing body. This vitally important right enables the people to directly support or reject both the 'collective' (national) political body, AND their own local representative member of Parliament. If I, as an ordinary member of the public, with no specialist knowledge, can discover from authoritative, respected independent sources, this most serious CRISIS in both the democratic systems and government actions and their consequences upon the nation's peoples, and then see that about one third of all those eligible to vote do not do so, then all future 'bad' government decisions can be laid firmly at their feet! You will get 'the government you deserve' and democracy will continue to decline!

Let me remind you of the piece of wisdom given to us in Britain, many, many years ago (introduction entitled 'The Social Contract'). Have you not noticed how the government in power always starts to appear to be giving 'rewards' to us the voters, for a time before a general election? 'Things are getting better' is the theme.

It is just blatant advertising to earn a few more votes to keep the present governing party in power. IGNORE IT! Look at the national situation during the WHOLE of their term of office. THEN DECIDE.

Please, please, take more interest in FACTS (not propaganda/'politic speak'), then form your OWN opinion, make your own choice. Then VOTE!

Democracy Restoration: Worldwide standards

So, we now have many evidential truths of the problem of 'worldwide un-democracy', and the problem of lessening democracy in 'developed' nations. One of the many consequences of this situation, which affect the more 'civilised' parts of the world, is the problem of refugees. Many, most commendable organisations carry out hundreds, perhaps thousands, of voluntary help actions to send direct help to oppressed peoples throughout the world. All credit to them and long may they continue in their vitally important work. I hope they will forgive me therefore when it must be admitted two negative elements of their work. *Neither of which is their fault.* Firstly, we are dealing with the symptoms of the problem/disease ('no true democracy') rather than the cause (dictatorships) of the problem. Secondly, some proportion (I know not how much) of the charity funds never find their way to the oppressed people. Of course, there must be organisational cost for this work.

Provided this is reasonable, no problem. But some reports say that actual dictatorial regimes require to take a large slice of the supporting materials (food, clothing etc.) before allowing it to be distributed to those people they are intended for.

And then we see other consequences of the problem, in the form of hundreds and thousands of refugees literally risking their lives to escape into other countries, even neighbouring ones where a different form of dictatorship rules. There is one other unpleasant realism that must be accepted about refugees. (I hate having to say this.) It is this. Through no fault of their own, the people fleeing from their own nations are accustomed to the needs and habits of '*survival*' codes of actions, habits of dreadful levels of injustice, suffering appalling standards of cleanliness, ill health, poverty, awful housing and a total lack of protection. Again (through no fault of their own), they can sometimes, without realising it, 'export' these habits and standards to other countries in their role as refugees. On the other hand, they also bring in their talents, attributes and alternative ideas for the 'receiving nation's benefit'. One thing that must be made clear in considering this problem. If we substitute the word 'refugees' for 'immigrants' we can take a much more positive approach to this situation. Look around our own country. We are a multinational nation. The vast majority who have earned 'nationalisation' make tremendous contributions to the benefit of our nation. In no way, am I advocating support for the 'white supremacy extremists'. So long as we apply basic conditions for entry and population ratios, consistently, immigration is very positive policy. However, we MUST be consistent in our rules and standards. Let us not, for example, erect a Statue of Liberty welcoming oppressed people from other lands, on the east coast and then build a big whacking wall on the west coast denying access by other people! BUT let us not forget that our own UK nation is an island, and our land size is NOT growing. 2022, in an article in the *Guardian* newspaper (August) it was reported that 'the proportion of people seeking asylum in the UK whose claims have been granted has now reached a 32 year high, as figures show the number of Albanians crossing the channel in small boats has increased substantially over the last few months'. This is in addition to other immigrants arriving in the UK by other 'routes'.

Not convinced? Check out the statistics on the website 'Worldometer. Countries in the EU by population (and land size) 2023'. The following list records the seven largest EU nations with their land size and population density.

Country	Land size (km^2)	Density (Population/ km^2)
Germany	348,560	240
France	547,557	119
Italy	294,140	206
Spain	498,800	94
Greece	128,900	81
Bulgaria	108,560	64
United Kingdom	242,295	270

Conclusion? The UK is by far the most, overpopulated nation in the EU AND the present government is doing little to STOP this worsening even more. There must be some environmental limit to our human population total, related to our geographical land area. Otherwise, we will have decreasingly fewer green areas, woods and forests, more housing, factories, roads, shops, more atmospheric pollution and so on. Sorry, but we must be realistic! I suspect that the majority view of the UK people would want this this situation stopping NOW. Clearly the UK Government is not doing this!

The other hidden problem with uncontrolled immigration, which to my mind at least, as an ordinary citizen, is that my own nation's 'personality' is being forcefully changed in many 'questionable' ways. Standards of behaviour, our heritage, people's personalities, laws, priorities, education, 'clique divisions'. This is happening without our realising it. As my very dear grandfather once said in some conversation about why some national matter should not be changed, his simple reason was 'Because we are British!' A bit racist you might think. Well, I am not so sure. In a recent discussion with an old friend of mine, who has spent a lifetime analysing crime statistics and anti-social behaviour, I was arguing that immigration was quite beneficial to the UK in that we were receiving large numbers of various professionally trained people from dictatorship-led nations and war situations. He raised a point which alarmed me somewhat. His question was 'Will unreserved immigration from a wide variety of different nations and cultures affect the UK's own habits, customs and personality adversely?' At the time I thought not. Now, I am not that sure. I am very proud of the character, standards of behaviour, personality and the 'British way of life' and culture. In my view there are signs that uncontrolled immigration, apart from the growing disproportionate (EU) aspect above can have an adverse effect upon the British way of life. We should accept the benefits of immigration, but they must accept the proverb, 'when in Rome, do as the Romans do'.

Many countries, to their credit, have ways of dealing with this situation. Refugee camps are one such way. I, as an ordinary citizen in a (fairly) democratic nation, want to emphasise, again, that we are failing to deal with the root cause of the problem. Wholly dysfunctional government in the country that the refugees are fleeing from.

So, if this is the problem. What is the remedy? In a nutshell we need to focus upon the root cause and deal with the fault within the country concerned. Or put another way, as we take in immigrants that satisfy reasonable conditions, we should, somehow, export our standards, laws, democracy, health, education, justice, etc. to the countries that create 'refugees' in the first place. A two-way deal, giving benefit to 'both sides'. But this must be conditional by taking actions directly against the 'elite'/dictatorship of the country concerned, by ways perhaps determined by the United Nations. Recall. 'If attacked by a giant, kill the head!' (i.e., The Refugees' own nation's leadership).

With my limited experience of governmental activity at the lowest of levels, my view is that we already operate the principles of a worldwide remedy at the 'lowest levels' of our own government structure. It is this. In, say, the educational and health forms of public services in the UK, the performance is measured using a relevant criterion which gives a yardstick of performance in various aspects of the particular service. In health matters, this might be waiting times of patients, number of beds available, performance of medical staff, costs of services and so on. In education, the criteria might be the ratio of teachers to pupils, examination success ratios, schools' managerial standards, etc. These standards are regularly monitored by an independent, non-political professional group. Where an establishment fails consistently to meet the previously defined standards, the establishment is declared to be 'dysfunctional and in need of special measures'. Some readers will be familiar with this kind of activity. Once an establishment has been declared as 'in need' some, or all, of the management role is taken over by an outside experienced and professional body which in my view must be non-commercial and non-political. OK, this system works for routine cases of local public services. My point is this. There is no reason why these principles of dealing with internal cases of a nation's internal problems cannot be applied worldwide, where dictatorship clearly prevents democracy, so causing the problems described above.

OK, let's 'play around' with this concept for a while. Here is a description that will enrage many, many people! 'Controlled, monitored, and professionally managed colonisation of a nation, declared by the UN, as "in need of special measures", for one generation (20 years), by a small coalition of neutral, developed nations, appointed and supervised by the UN.' In my ignorance, it might be that something along these lines already happens. If so, all well and good. If not, let us develop this theme a little more. Again, ignoring the howls of protest, effectively, this means that a nation loses its power of self-government for a specified period but not to a single neighbouring nation. (Let's not do a 'EU' type of 'power acquisition'!) How would we do this? Again, in very simplistic terms, one order of events might be as follows.

- The United Nations determines universally accepted criteria, which defines a nation as undemocratic, with dysfunctional governmental internal control, where people suffer appalling living conditions, hunger, famine, injustice, cruelty and oppression. If, in my ignorance, this has already been done, OK! Has it recently been reviewed, however?
- Where there is clear and verifiable evidence showing that much of this criteria exists, United Nations independent, professional assessors (with adequate protection) investigates the DETAILED position and submits a full report to the UN assembly.
- If the report shows that the UN criteria conditions do exist, the assembly makes a worldwide declaration of 'in need of extensive special measures' against the nation concerned. This is followed by detailing the specific action needed to be taken, over a certain period, by the nation, itself. This serves as a warning that failure to meet the UN requirements may result in the UN assembly considering the option of taking over, either full or partial governmental responsibility from the present administration,

specifying the period involved, and the detailed objectives of the work to be done.

- If the nation fails to meet the UN requirements, after the agreed period of time, as evidenced by UN assessors, the UN appoints an 'acting coalition government' consisting of independent, non-political, professional persons from other nations, backed up by supporting military, police, technical, scientific, legal and governmental officer 'resources' from the UN and also from the actual nation concerned. They effectively remove and replace most of the nation's governmental structure for a UN body for a specified period of time. (Think this is a step too far? Look again at what is happening NOW in a previous chapter).

- The 'coalition nations' then takes over as 'acting government'. Considering the large commitment for this task, the coalition would be permitted to extract UN defined benefits from the country's own resources, providing they are able to show real genuine progress in putting specific things right. UN assessors would continue their checks throughout this situation, which might be for periods of 10, 20 years or so. This would involve training and educating the nation's own people in appropriate rebuilding disciplines, health, basic laws and progressively developing democratic standards, enshrined by the nation's laws.

- As the nation concerned continues to improve, governmental power is progressively returned to the nation's own people.

I am already hearing the howls of protest from those who have their own vested interest in preventing this and other similar remedies. All these should be heard, provided they all declare clearly and honestly their religious, political and or financial interests, beforehand.

The benefits of such a plan could be enormous, permanently internally and worldwide. In the UK, we are still even now, enjoying some of the benefits of 'colonialism' provided by the Romans! I often choose to travel along roads provided by the Romans through some beautiful English countryside. The English language is a worldwide means of communication. Nations copy other nations in many areas, and so on. 'Colonialism' is not all bad, particularly if it is independently, non-politically, professionally, managed and monitored and benefits the nation's own people!

I read, and noted somewhere (I cannot remember where), an exceptionally vital principal. 'Societies throughout the world's nations, need to reorganise their PRIORITIES based upon a considerably more favourable element of people's lives, and a high regard to maintaining all the environmental elements of the whole planet'. To whoever the writer was, all credit for defining, so accurately, an essential rule for this (currently) beautiful world of ours! It would be one vitally important standard for 'UN intervention', in an oppressed, undemocratic nation.

Geographical (political) attempts of 'grouping' of separate nations.

Over the last century, one of the most appalling aspects of the human population is the continuing pursuit of power by leaders of existing nations over neighbouring nations. Consider, if you will, just the following incidents.

- First World War. A 'crown prince(?)' is assassinated in a small/medium size nation in Europe. This is followed by a succession of countries forming allegiances and starting the First World War. All started by the nations' 'elite'. Is this not madness!
- Second World War. Germany invades Poland (I know not why). Straight away, other nations throughout the whole world join in this war, which ended with the first use of nuclear weapons.
- European Union nations CAN decide to join in a group called say, a 'common market'. BUT, As shown earlier, the governmental internal powers of the joining nations SHOULD NOT have their powers progressively stripped away, and transferred to some central bureaucratic authority. A defensive pact coordinated scientific research; friendship 'twinning' activities are more positive kinds of bonding.
- China, already having the largest nation in the world continue in expansion over many years, NOW with eyes on Taiwan. The previous 'nation' was Hong Kong. This is NOT the way to have

positive partnerships and grouping of separate nations.

- Russia, again (second?) largest nation, is currently (2021/2) invading neighbouring Ukraine. (Could this be the start of the 'Third World War'?). The bottom line, in the eyes of increasing numbers of people from other nations, is being simply described as the pursuit of increased personal power by various parts of one nation's 'elite classes', over other nations.

There is, in practice, nothing wrong in the principal of nations forming positive, alliances with neighbouring nations. But in practice it always seems to end up the same way. Reduced 'real' democracy for the nations peoples, and more power for political dictators and bureaucracies. This must stop, unless the PEOPLE of both nations, by a free and open referendum, vote in support!

The remedy has already been showed to us by the original concept in Europe for the 'common market'. We saw in a previous chapter why this failed. Based on what we have learned from that experience, why cannot the world's nations still form alliances with neighbouring nations, but still protect the basic principles of democracy. Ultimate power remaining with the nation's own people. In my view a 'coalition' of neighbouring nations CAN be formed by accepting the following – say – six principals.

1. Trade. Preferential/beneficial deals within the 'coalition', and joint exporting to the outside world.
2. Truly beneficial scientific research and development co-ordination between universities, and other agencies searching for new means and improvements environmentally, commercially, health, education etc.
3. Friendship bonds between communities. Twinning groups, holidays and 'U3A' activities.
4. Genuine 'levelling up' policies. Cost of living, education, health, workers' rights.
5. Democracy development. Joint reviews, regular 'market surveys' of people's concerns and wishes. Increasing standards of transparency with the increased use of people's referendums.
6. Defence and law and order. Secure boundaries. Threats to one nation amounts to threats to the whole coalition (e.g., NATO). High level of common standards in all legal areas.

These are just examples of the way to develop support and friendship without losing any aspect of an individual nations own democratic standards.

The World's 'War' Problem

Finally, in respect of 'world level democracy' we MUST deal with the question of WARS. As has been said previously, since mankind has developed the most awful weapons as mass destruction, wars now HAVE to be prevented for the simple reason of 'whole world preservation!' What has happened in the past cannot be changed. What happens in the future MUST be controlled. A worldwide simple convention needs unreserved adoption. No nation may invade, with warlike actions, another nation, unless there is clear and indisputable evidence of a FIRST 'strike' (as defined by the UN), by the (second named) nation.

We should NOT forget, that when the facts originally emerged about the awful result of using 'weapons of mass destruction' (WMD's), in London there were mass demonstrations by ordinary people entitled 'BAN THE BOMB'. This was a clear demand for all nations to carry out this prohibition. Did any government listen to the voice of the people? NO. The excuse was 'if XYZ nation has the bomb, we need them to for self-defence'.

Again, the voice of the world's people was wholly ignored.

We have already seen earlier who suffers the most from wars, and who funds the enormous financial costs of wars? (The world's people.) And secondly, who decides upon HOW, WHY and WHEN to start a war? The answers are obvious and cannot be denied. So far as who decides? is concerned, it is the various kinds of 'elitist' classes (political, religious, commercial) in the world. So far as WHO pays most is concerned, it is the millions (? billions) of the worlds PEOPLE who gives their LIVES and serious injuries, and THEN have to spend many, many years thereafter actually paying for the enormous financial costs of wars. I often hear the claim that we are still, in many ways, paying for the Second World War. Is this true? Do we ever see the 'elite classes' on the front lines of wars? Do we see any benefit to the world's environment, from wars?

It is time for ALL people of all nations, to start to say collectively, 'NO!' TO ANY ATTEMPT TO 'START' A WAR AGAINST ANY OTHER NATION. This can only be done by a growing worldwide convention of ALL people throughout the world demanding 'No FIRST warlike strike against any other nation'. This would not take away a nation's right to DEFEND itself from a 'first strike'. The worlds peoples have paid enough in the fights created, entirely, for the personal power of the elite classes!

In my view, the United Nations, being presently the only legitimate world governing body (by a, say, 75% vote), would determine that a warlike invasion, by one nation against another nation, to be wholly unacceptable, unjustified and undemocratic. This would be followed by a worldwide ban upon all economic, fiscal trading (particularly weapons) to the invading nation for a given period. If this does not stop the war, then, again under the control of the UN, and ONLY then, other non-involved nations would be called upon to take actions specifically aimed at the invading nation's governing leadership. In the 'current' war crisis (Russia invading the Ukraine) I fully support the actions of nations who limit their response of supporting the Ukraine by 'defensive (nonnuclear) weaponry' together with extensive 'economic' measure against Russia's 'elite' classes'. (As the saying goes, 'if you are attacked by a giant, kill the head'!) I know there would be problems with this kind of response. But the basic principal of stopping wars by dictatorship regimes against other nations, 'without just cause', HAS TO BE ACCEPTED, DEFINED, ADOPTED AND APPLIED, for the sake of the whole world.

It is, of course, true that UN members come from all nations, throughout the world, but 'democracy' is heavily dependent upon the 'will of the majority'. Members are still able to vote for or against motions, or 'declare an interest' and abstain from voting. Nonetheless, a majority decision can still be taken, which ALL members must accept.

Finally on this subject of the decline of democracy worldwide, at the time of drafting this chapter (Feb. 2022) Russia's premier Putin is currently proving that all the concerns of authoritative writers telling us that democracy is failing and that this is a very serious matter are dead on correct! Firstly, however, let us remember again, the media's 'addiction' for 'sensationalism', as already defined previously and some level of presumption must be given that 'not all' media claims are totally accurate. In this case, however, I think we can presume that as there is a general consistency amongst all media headlines, we can accept that we are being given a fairly accurate picture of the truth.

I would like to offer a message to, like myself, 'ordinary' (no disrespect) citizens in Russia. It is this. In 1917, your past family generations RIGHTLY rose and defeated the TZARIST (royalty) dictatorship and brought in 'socialism' (which when applied democratically is a good form of government). Your forebears, family generations, gave their very lives to defeat that form of dictatorship. How would their family spirits view YOUR actions now? Who, of you, is paying money for this war, who is being killed and seriously injured in this war? Please, as for all other nations, rise up again and fully reinstate YOUR socialistic democratic rights to have YOUR say in government policies, and to be at peace with all your neighbouring nations, and the world! (And perhaps with the spirits of your own ancestors.) I know, in your hearts, you would wish this. Well, so do we!

The most important and essential point is this. No nation's leader should have the right to start a war, just on their own prejudices and personal power ambitions, acting only with the approval of a few ('arse licking') personal supporters who themselves are simply 'politically ambitious' (apologies again for my obscenities). We are talking about dictatorships gaining more and more POWER. This must stop! The only 'excuse' for this wholesale invasion is that the Ukraine government was considering joining NATO (North Atlantic Treaty Organisation) simply as a means of maintaining and protecting their own sovereignty and democracy. Yes, against Russian oppression. All Putin has done is demonstrate that the Ukrainian fears were entirely justified. E.g., An armoured Russian convoy estimated to be 40 miles long entering Ukraine. Thousands more refugees fleeing the nation. Were the Russian PEOPLE consulted before the invasion? NO. Is this an isolated case for Russia? NO. Does China, another strong socialist nation, take other expansionist actions? POSSIBLY. (Hong Kong, Taiwan.) Germany? Invasion of Poland, resulting in you know what. This kind of action must STOP. Otherwise get ready, people, for that SUDDEN, out of the blue FIREBALL! For most of the world.

Democracy, throughout the whole world is fraught with politicians and nations' leaders who are adept at 'talking the talk', making agreements that sounds good, then walking away claiming they have achieved something that warrants them staying in power. Using, again today's example of the Russian INVASION (!) of Ukraine. Whatever happened to the 1949 'Geneva Convention' relating to 'rules of war'? This was an internationally agreed treaty, specifically with the aim of protecting prisoners of war, aid workers, medical professionals and people who can no longer fight. The treaty comprised of four conventions, the 'fourth' convention specifically, protects civilians, including people in occupied territory and buildings. So my question is this. Why are we now seeing so many pictures of bombed residential areas and homeless people in the Ukraine, caused by artillery bombardment from adjoining locations? Is it any wonder that there is a worldwide growing distrust of many nations' governments?

So, what can learn from this latest experience of oligarchy? Some measures are put forward earlier in this chapter. But the threat still remains. (Weapons of mass destruction.) What might be a remedy for this? A remedy that takes away from the world's dictators and 'elite' a kind of 'tool' to help them stay in power AND extend their power. The remedy, to my mind, is contained in the subject, already defined earlier. Social responsibility. Who created weapons of mass destruction in the first place? It has to be said, it was the world's scientific community. If we accept this statement, without going into all the reasons and excuses for this simple fact, I say, it is perfectly reasonable to call upon the whole world's scientific community, under the terms of social responsibility, to develop a way of destroying all forms of these weapons (nuclear, chemical, biological), laughingly, still described as a nuclear 'deterrents' (another 'politicisation' of the truth). Did I read somewhere that the largest holder in the whole world of nuclear bombs and missiles is Russia? I also remember reading somewhere of what seemed to be a somewhat outrageous claim that a new generation of weapons are being designed called 'killer robots'. Does this mean that in future we will not need 'human' armies to fight for greater power for the world 'elite'? Whether true or not, THIS HAS GOT TO STOP! So, my plea to the world's scientific community is to find the courage to ignore the demands of the 'elite' TO PROVIDE MORE AND MORE WEAPONS IN ORDER FOR THEM TO ACQUIRE MORE PERSONAL POWER and find a genuine deterrent, freely available to the whole world, to destroy or neutralise all weapons of mass destruction, the minute they are launched or otherwise released. If you succeed in doing this, your 'crime' in firstly developing these weapons can be forgiven; you will have made a real contribution to restoring power to the people (democracy); oh, and 'incidentally', you will have saved our beautiful world from wholesale destruction. A rather important REMEDY do you not think? Finally, your biggest 'enemy' in doing this work will, actually, be your own governing body, who will continue to press you to give them more 'tools' with which to use in acquiring more personal power. You are going to have to find a way round this, for all our sakes. Is it not possible to argue that if you succeed in finding these kinds of DEFENCES against THESE weapons of mass destruction, you are, in fact, making your nation much safer and more secure (as well as the 'elite', as well!?).

The Role and Purpose of Science and Technology

Yet again, we need to emphasise the point that, from the outset, science and technology have produced so many improvements and developments that benefit both the whole world environment, and all living things. Few people would argue against this notion. However, for the sake of fairness, we have to look at the negative side of 'science and technology' i.e., is 'the continuous pursuit of excellence' WHOLLY applied. Sadly, there IS a 'downside'. My own selection of 'downside' actions of science is the following.

- The development of weapons of mass destruction.
- The abuse of environmental resources (coal, gas, oil, forests, minerals).
- Genetic engineering of living things.
- Robotics.
- Elimination of personal privacy.
- Information technology.
- Unproven remedies in medicine.

- Pandering to the excessive demands of the 'elite'.
- Ignoring worldwide rules for controlling and monitoring scientific development and research (UN resolution 43, use of science for real positive benefits).
- Insufficient verification of new 'discoveries', leading to erroneous and faulty conclusions (and again, pressure from 'elite commercialism').

If the protocol for scientific development ('the pursuit of excellence') still stands, remedies such as the following might be considered.

- Review and strengthen the UN world standards by requiring increased investigations into ALL the consequences of new discoveries.
- Application of all the principals of social responsibility.
- Economic 'punishments' (e.g., a large environment TAX).
- Economic 'rewards' for proven near perfect scientific developments.
- Information technologies must be slowed down, in order that the benefits and risks can be accurately evaluated beforehand and made more understandable to all people.

Once again, applying the principal quoted by an unknown source (to development) simply to stress a condition applicable to scientific development. 'Societies throughout the world's nations, need to reorganise their PRIORITIES based upon a considerably more favourable element of people's lives, and a high regard to maintaining all the environmental elements of the whole planet'.

From a history of refining stronger swords in the world's history of wars, to the development of today's awful weapons of mass destruction, my plea to the scientific communities of the world is to STOP developing things that only give more power to nation leaders (who are only interested in using your discoveries to increase their level of personal power and influence). In other words, to use your talents and abilities only to improve the world's environment and all life forms on the beautiful world of ours.

Banks and financial institutions: both the world and the UK

Lastly in respect of worldwide aspects of democracy, but still very important, is MONEY, and the question of how the world, and individual nations can, from a monetary point of view, vastly improve the circumstances of democracy, people's lives and the whole world environment. Apart from the 'dictatorship elite' element, the gross and obnoxious inequality in the world's billionaires and the people's considerably lower levels of 'living' make up the most powerful, combined enemy of democracy. Our (the people's) problem is how to rectify this appalling level of inequality and injustice. I confess, I do not know. The conceptual remedy is for the world's fair minded financial experts who strongly believe in democracy restoration, to draw up a *worldwide FINANCIAL social responsibility charter/convention, which encompasses the quotation (from an unknown source)* repeated, for the sake of emphasis, above.

The previous chapter relating to the 'austerity' aspect showed that, by the government of the day, in the UK, allowing the nation's banks free rein to manage fiscal policies, it became an absolute disaster for the people, but increased the number and wealth, of both 'millionaires' AND 'billionaires'! Let us all, at least, start this move by getting rid of our debts and reducing one 'life blood' (grotesque levels of interest charges) of the obscenely rich classes. But, as already has been said, the real remedy is in the hands of democratic minded financiers and economists to offer new ways to us, the people, upon how to force the implementation of FINANCIAL social responsibility POLICIES, based upon 'nation's priorities' as defined above.

I repeat, yet again, how we saw in an earlier chapter how austerity damn near ruined the UK's whole economy yet made 'the ELITE' very happy indeed. This is a major international and national problem, for the whole world, and needs extensive changes and controls. Again, justifying the use of the word 'CRISIS' in this book's title.

I believe that one remedy MUST be considered. It is a 'wealth tax', nationally and worldwide upon the easily identified 'billionaires' (and in some cases, the 'trillionaires') to reduce worldwide debt and to rectify at least some of the aspects of the global environmental crisis. The grotesque amount of inequality HAS TO BE CORRECTED, in a way that benefits the whole world, its environment and its people,

United Kingdom: Democracy Restoration and Strengthening

Parliament members: people's surgeries

Again, let us start by defining 'what are MP's surgeries'. My computer tells me MPs usually hold surgeries ONCE or TWICE a week, often on a Friday or Saturday. They are sessions where MPs can invite their constituents to make appointments to meet their them to discuss issues affecting them or problems they are facing. They are held in a public library or other 'public buildings', within their constituency. Each MP has a different way of operating their surgeries. They might be just a simple 'drop-in session' or may allocate appointment times for each constituent. This is where there is serious fault with the framework of their prime task and duty to 'represent their constituents'.

In my view/perspective, elected MPs should be required by law to hold and attend monthly surgeries in their constituencies. Again, according to Wikipedia 'it is up to each MP to decide whether they have any surgeries at all and if so, how many and in what location'. If this is so, it is quite disgraceful! How many people know who their MP is? How many people know when and where 'surgeries' are held? When is the ONLY time an MP (or often, their 'helpers'), visit their constituents? (We all know the answer to these questions!) Even the description 'their constituents' raises a question in my mind in respect of MPs who reside WELL OUTSIDE their constituencies.

If a national government becomes 'unfit for purpose' and 'in need of special measures' – (public sector terminology) – then power to determine essential national policies should be returned to the nation's people in various ways and in particular circumstances. 'Various ways' means referendums, public petitions and 'extraordinary' general elections (following, for instance, an overwhelming support from people in an open public petition). 'Particular circumstances' need to be clearly defined, such as 'warlike circumstances', 'serious economic decline', 'vital environmental problems', 'standards of conduct/ behaviour' and 'international relations'.

The bottom line is this. 'Representing people's needs, wishes and opinions, is an essential, unavoidable, absolute requirement'. The whole process needs reorganising, employing the full independent OPEN use of both personal contact and information technology, which enables communications UPWARDS, and actions taken and/or results achieved for the people, rather than dancing attendance to the whims and preferences of contributing 'lobby' groups and buying votes using public money. Governments should be required, by law, to issue monthly public notices of meetings, giving the date, time and location, and giving the people full rights to attend, allowing attending members of the public to raise issues and ask questions. local councils are required to publish 'websites' giving much information upon actions taken and to publish approved full copies of the meeting minutes (records of meetings decisions) and the detailed annual accounts showing how every penny of the public's council tax payments has been spent. So, in both theory and practice, MPs have, far and away, less contact with the constituents who elected them (and from whom come all public funds!). How the hell can they represent the views and concerns of their constituents? Yet again, the quotation I made in this book's introduction page (Jeanne-Jacques) made nearly four hundred years ago is shown to be completely accurate still TODAY. (So, Guy Fawkes was right then!) I accept that some issues raised by members of the public, are not 'resolvable' by the MP. If this is the case, at least explain why. But, nonetheless, all issues raised by constituents, represent symptoms of real concerns and problems, deserve consideration AND recording. There HAS to be a centralised system ('IT', I hate to have to admit it!) but recall an earlier comment. 'IT' can be a two-edged sword of recording ALL people's questions, concerns and complaints, fully analysed statistically, by an independent, non-political body AND THEN MADE public, in the UK Government library.

Finally on this subject, it surprises me that little seems to be done in carrying out independent professional surveys of people's wishes nationally and needs, and then compared this with the governments actual actions, with the results given due publicity by the media. (My research continues!) This would be an excellent measure of the representativeness of any government in any nation.

The UK's Government's 'House of Lords'

One of the remedies for restoring democracy in the UK (which I think is attracting an increasing amount of public support), is the complete closure of the House of Lords. A 'revolutionary' level of action, admittedly, needing substantial evidence to justify this decision. This view has been around for some time now, and is a matter long overdue, for NATIONAL consideration. This should not be too difficult to do. Since ALL the costs of the House of Lords (I will not go into the payments to 'their lordships' again!) come from the public funds (OUR TAXES), are we not entitled to have a say upon whether we want to keep the House of Lords, by a full and public REFERENDUM? (Shock horror!). Anyway, back to the facts.

Firstly, I have extracted from the 'Parliament UK' website statistics upon the current (2021) membership of the House of Lords by 'political party/group'. My 'abacus bead frame' (!) tells me that, of the total number of 'peers' (lords) (778), 704 come from the 'four' main political parties, being 243 Conservative, 183 'cross bench' (political others'), 182 Labour and 96 Liberal Democrats. A very few come from 'non-political sources (e.g., bishops etc.), All of the political groups of peers arise from nominations by political leaders. The 'official line' (duty) of peers is to use their professional experience (political experience) to carry out the work of the House of Lords (defined in an earlier chapter, 'Structure of the UK Government'). One of which is to monitor, and comment upon the work of the 'Lower' House (of Commons). Let us recall, all of these lifetime appointments owe their new (exceedingly high) 'lifestyle' to political parties. Where do you think their loyalties lie? To us, perhaps, the actual creators of all public funds that give them a lavish level of living – for life! To my mind, they are only appointed to the House of Lords for 'past political' work as a reward (or even possibly to get rid of them because of past political misdemeanours!). ('He who pays the piper, calls the tune'?) We should not forget either that being a 'lord' greatly assists them to earn 'a bob or two extras' from outside 'interests and appointments'. How much information do we know of these 'perks' I ask? See the next but one paragraph.

Yet again, we see another glaring example of inequality of standards amongst the 'highest' levels of government, and the 'lowest levels'. Our local councillors have a statutory duty to declare 'pecuniary' interests' (principally financial, managerial) when certain matters are debated in meetings. They then take no part in the discussions or decisions. Detailed guidance is given in operating this rule. It is a test question. To quote the guideline, 'Would a member of the public, knowing all the circumstances of the particular case, reasonably believe that the personal interests were so significant, that (the councillor's) decisions (comments) on the matter would be affected ('influenced') by it'. A good standard, created by Parliament for local councils but not for the government itself, in my view. So here is the question. Having been GIVEN a lavish lifestyle for life by a political party, where do you think their loyalties lie? There is a very informative article on this very subject issued by the 'Electoral Reform Society' entitled 'Unelected Aristocrats'. It was on the web. If you can, have a read of this.

At the time of writing this chapter (November 2021), there was a growing demand for peers to be forced to declare all the kinds of 'extra perks'. To quote from one article, 'peers, the Upper House, may be required to record personal interests involving foreign investments, under "transparency laws", following worries over Russian/Chinese influence in British politics' (To which

I start singing 'We've heard it all before, we've heard it all before, etc.') Did it happen in 2019? Did it happen in 2020? Did it happen in 2021? Will it happen in 2022? I leave you to vote your response if a responsible independent association was willing to provide a 'people's referendum' on the web. Which is one of the recommendations in this book.

Coalition governments

Let me start by expressing my own opinion. I like the concept of coalition governments, but with new standards and conditions. The trouble these days following an indecisive general election result, they are only formed to keep a major political group in power with minor changes to their election manifesto. Do I recall correctly that some time ago, in the recent past, the Conservative Party once remained in power by forming a coalition arrangement with the DUP, and that during this period, more national funds were allocated to Northern Ireland? If this was not the case, I apologise. If my memory is, however, fairly accurate, I would not criticise the DUP for getting more benefit for their community. They would only be acting for their people interests. However (again presuming my memory is reasonably accurate), is it not a deplorable principal for a large political party to 'BUY' support for staying in power, from public funds?

Limiting the number of 'political parties' standing for general elections

Readers will recall from the earlier chapter 'The Present-Day Government Structure in the UK', the rather long list of 'parties' standing for election in the 2019 general election (i.e., 58 out of 68). In my perspective, the nation's 'democracy level' would be improved if this list was the subject of two additional limitations. Firstly, if a 'party' fails to get less than a specified low minimum of votes at a general election, they would not be able to stand at the next general election. This is already the rule in another truly democratic nation. Secondly, a political 'party' that only stands for purely 'local' issues would not be able to stand, simply because the general election is for the national government, mainly concerned with national issues.

Inconclusive general election results

So, what standards/conditions would I call for when a general election fails to result in a 'working majority' and the question of a coalition becomes a possibility. I would expect that the two separate political parties would – quickly – integrate their separate election manifestos, not necessarily equally, but proportionally, based upon percentage votes cast by the electorate for each party. Before the final decision is made, I would expect the proposed, amended joint manifesto would be made completely public (on the web, not by the prejudiced media). The benefit, democratically speaking, would show the electorate that public funds are to be spent more in accordance with the people's wishes as expressed by their votes in support of the original party's manifestos.

Increasing the nation's people's control in MAJOR issues

To my mind, there is one (surprising) criterion for basic democracy, which I have not found in any of the universal interpretations. It is that issues of the highest national importance should only be decided by the nation's people. Two examples immediately spring to mind. Going to war with another nation, and MAJOR economic policies. Both issues have a major impact on people's lives (but rarely on the lives of the decision makers!) In the case of a 'war' scenario (as discussed in the earlier section, in this chapter), it would have to be a worldwide standard that before starting a new war, a nation's own governing body would be required to hold a proper and fair referendum put to that nation's people, with statutory conditions protecting the people's rights to express a view and with independent controls upon bullying voters to vote in a certain way. The only exception to this worldwide condition, is to maintain the right of immediate self-defence following an unjustified attack by another nation who had not carried a people's referendum. In this case, intervention, controlled by the UN, by other nations would have to be considered, again as defined earlier.

In respect of major economic issues, which have a serious impact upon the people's livelihoods (e.g., 'austerity' measures, restrictions on people's working conditions, 'trading' wars), again a people's referendum is needed, but with alternatives, and clearly defined courses of action, for voters to choose from. The involvement by independent, non-political, economic advisory institutions would be required with their 'alternative courses of action' freely publicised for ALL people to see.

Finally, on this subject, I have previously argued for the phasing out of the House of Lords, because of their failure to hold the House of Commons 'to account'. (And also the dreadful waste of public money!) I personally do not have much confidence that this will happen soon. Nevertheless 'one day' it will have to happen. What then, we might ask? My answer would be that we focus on the main (failed) purpose of the Lords, to hold 'to account' the actions of the House of Commons. I would have one idea only. It is to establish a 'people's assembly' supported by THEIR OWN independent non-political, professional, related advisory institutions, with a large membership of 'ordinary' voters, chosen by 'lot', from the whole nation, in the same way the law courts juries are appointed, but for a specified period of time. True democracy would be seriously improved if, one day, such a change would happen. The 'people's assembly' with their own specialist, independent advisers would thus be able to 'consider the truth, the whole truth and nothing but the truth' and be much more able to 'hold to account' the actions of the House of Commons.

The role of the 'speaker' in the House of Commons

Anyone who has watched on TV, the debates in the House of Commons, particularly when political leaders (and others) are hurling offensive and intimidatory remarks at each other, you may have wondered who actually controls the debate and behaviour of leaders, and MPs? It is, of course, the 'speaker' of the House of Commons who sits in an elevated position at the front, facing both sides of the 'House' with the loud firm words of 'Order, order!' John Bercow was (to my mind), most able and adept at this, to the point of disfavour with political leaders. As I have already said. 'Sadly, he had to go.' However, the weakness, is that 'speakers' normally, apparently, have a political background and can thus be prejudiced, and not wholly respected by an opposite political party.

However, as can be openly viewed on the web, there is published a long and detailed 'code of conduct' for all

MPs which clearly specifies codes of conduct and behaviour, declarations of personal interest, roles and responsibilities of MPs and many other rules of conduct. The code is extensive, detailed and covers many different situations which are inherent and complex. So much so, that – in my view – one 'speaker', in front of a full house of 'Commons' (over 600 MPs), where much is being said and argued, is hopelessly inadequate to monitor actual and full compliance for all elements of the code. I believe the 'speaker' (and deputy 'speakers') should be a barrister (in law) – king's counsellor, appointed by and responsible to the nation's sovereign, on the advice of the Bar Counsel (barristers in law) and/or the UK law society. We can thus expect a much more competent, knowledgeable, extensive, independent, implementation of the governments code of conduct. This does not, in any way, reduce the power of government in all the respect of the government's role. That would be unchanged.

I believe that the speaker's role should then be made more authoritative in controlling debates and behaviour, assisted on either side with deputy speakers to provide support as needed. This need is important. A recent example of the current limited authority of the speaker under the current system was recorded on 'web news', *Evening Standard*, 25/2/22. I quote, 'Sir Lindsey Hoyle (speaker) has URGED (!) the government "Chief Whip" to crack down on the level of shouting and barracking from Conservative MPs during the prime minister's question time. (When other MPs can ask direct questions of the PM). A Green Party MP was interrupted on several occasions, as she tried to ask the PM About Russian interference in the UK (2019) general elections.' Do we not think that we, the people, also have a right to know the truth in this kind of case? Do we not think there is an urgent need for proper standards of debate to be strongly enforced?

One recent (early March 2023) absolutely appalled me. This was a visually recorded scene and broadcast on TV, showing a MOB fight amongst middle aged men in a closed room. A drunken mob brawl perhaps by unruly men who should know better? The room was situated, apparently, in a room somewhere in the Parliamentary buildings, BY SOME 30 members of Parliament! I sat appalled and watched it with my own eyes. Was this appalling incident investigated and those guilty for starting it brought to justice? Not as yet!

The speaker's role MUST be strengthened in that he/she would not be answerable to political leaders, but perhaps direct to the nation's sovereign who would have the power to refer a case to the House of Lords (or, as I would prefer), to a replaced 'people's assembly'.

Extension of 'referendum consultations'

Let us remind ourselves of the circumstances of the 'Brexit referendum' Here we had a very rare occasion where a government decided during their term of office to consult the voters upon whether an important national issue. This was to remain in the 'EU' or leave. It is not an unreasonable opinion to have that the government, who wanted to 'stay', hoped that the people would support this option of remaining. Shock, horror! A narrow but clear majority voted OUT. This was followed by clumsy and obvious attempts to delay the action, hoping that different circumstances might arise giving an excuse to ignore the people's decision. (Sadly, this has been, in the past, a typical political 'tactic' when an 'inconvenient truth' or incident, comes out into the open) This did not happen. Result? 2019 general election. The new1 Leader of the Conservative Party (Boris Johnson), with his hand on his heart (?!) promised to carry out the people's wishes, and to be fair, he did exactly that and the UK became an independent nation once again.

My point is this. On national vital issues, like retaining our independence and democracy levels, the people have a right to be consulted. Not a difficult task at all with (for once!) modern information technology. An important test of democracy levels would be 'passed'. If we also copied one European nation's law, relating to freedom to hold and recognise, 'people's petitions' (subject to certain conditions being complied with). If this rule was applied in the UK its position on the of world's level of democracy would go up and such a standard would vastly improve the democratic requirement of 'upward influence'.

(Once again perhaps we could check how the 'lower' tiers of government work in these kinds of cases and what controls THEY use, 'voters satisfaction levels upon local public services'. Local councils may thus be able to tell the government how THEY should function, rather than the other way round!)

Using the UK people's abilities and collective wisdom

I have already offered my view on this very subject relating to the replacement of the UK's House of Lords. This view originates from many hours of research from many different sources of responsible and accurate information supporting the notion of 'the CRISIS of declining democracy'. These sources need a damn sight more publicity by the media than headline news about such matters I listed in my chapter upon the freedom of the press, upon one day's headlines from that day's morning papers. By giving much more publicity to the kind of reference sources from those I have already quoted, AND others, the 'collective wisdom of a nations people's' would be even more enriched and if we could persuade more voters to exercise their (VITAL) rights to vote at elections, the benefits of increased democracy (in all nations) would benefit the whole world.

One other remedy to improve democracy argued, 'Let the scientists make the mistakes.' Fair point, and to be honest, one other idea, which I am sure could help in the most urgent need for democracy restoration. (Most political groups will absolutely hate this idea!) This would allow well reputed professionals, academics and scientists, much more influence in the whole process of 'repairing' our very faulty democracy systems and to 'audit' important, specified, government policies. By far, their whole professional lives are dedicated to independent, truthful and verified evidence in all matters affecting our world's environment. One of their prime aims is 'the pursuit of excellence'. Such a body would have its principal work in auditing all government decisions alongside the 'vital principal' recorded earlier 'societies throughout the world need to...', and to monitor the elected governments 'manifestos' published during their election to office showing their manifesto promises, alongside ACTUAL results. This professional body would be made up of lawyers/barristers, wholly independent financiers/accountants and as, when necessary, scientists and other professionals of relevant disciplines. They should not have any power to make national policy decisions, but their knowledge, personal standards and talents at identifying truisms and ideas for improvements, with absolutely NO 'politicisation' of various circumstances, would uncover realistic truths and ways to improve, maintain and develop democracy, as chosen by the collective wisdom of the people. Their task is to identify government actions which are seriously contrary to the two criteria defined above, and to openly publish a full report upon their findings, for the people to judge, possibly by (for example) the use of referendums. If such a referendum shows a pronounced people's conclusion, the government would be under an obligation to apply the people's wishes, or show a bloody good reason, why NOT! Such a system would satisfy the rule 'government BY the people, FOR the people (and the environment)'. In an 'IT opinion' published on the web (Feb. 2022) 'commercialism and the pursuit of power' is a damn sight more guilty. Yet again, it is the collective wisdom of the people that would reduce this risk.

Restoring the people's rights to fight the growing element of 'oligarchy'

We have two clear examples of the UK Government's attempts to reduce the rights of working people to act against wholly unjust restrictions imposed upon freedom of expression, and their employment rights. Currently (2022) the government is seriously considering taking away the basic rights of public demonstrations against prejudicial national policies. The current proposal, called the 'The Police Act' ('Bill') effectively takes away almost all the rights of people to demonstrate, and extends the powers of the (already understaffed) police to ban people from expressing justified opposition against government actions. The 'excuse' I am told is to exaggerate incidents of unruly behaviour to reduce people's rights of public expressions of their concerns. (Unruly behaviour is not necessary, there are better ways to demonstrate acting within existing laws.) Do not the police authorities themselves realise they are being used purely as a 'political' weapon, against people, rather than their principal objective of fighting crime against people? Even the 'Upper House' (House of Lords) has opposed this proposal!

Another matter which may have not been noticed by us the people. Have we not noticed that justified strikes by workers against employers oppressive and unfair practices (wage reductions, redundancies, working conditions etc.) are now, virtually 'a thing of the past'? This situation was caused, many years ago, by the government (again), laying down difficult to meet conditions for strike action, because they claimed that 'trade union dictators' were forcing workers to strike as a weapon against the government. Which I know was total rubbish, because whenever a strike occurred it was after the workers, in a free and properly organised election, voted overwhelmingly to take strike action! But that rarely got publicised by the media!

Remedy? Simple. Fully reinstate/maintain BOTH rights (workers' rights, and demonstrations). But this would require fair and just standards determined by a non-political body. This body would comprise of experts in appropriate disciplines (barristers, economists, independent industrialists, trade union officers and a people's 'jury'). Finally, I would make WAGES a direct and equal relationship with the increasing income of the 'elite' classes, be they commercial, governmental or dictatorships! Yet another 'remedy' for INEQUALITY.

UK Government's 'oligarchy' element (yet again): Parliamentary 'whips'

One aspect of an earlier chapter (Chapter 2) 'The UK's Current Structure', which to my mind is not immediately apparent to the UK's electorate, is the political systems of 'party whips'. A UK Parliament web page gives us the following definition. 'Whips are MPs or members of the House of Lords appointed by each party in Parliament to help organise their party's contribution to Parliamentary business. One of their responsibilities is making sure the maximum numbers of their parties members vote and vote the way their party wants.' This definition goes on. 'Three-line whips' (wording underlined by THREE lines in the whip's papers to all their party MPs) normally apply to 'major' events for significant future bills (government decisions). This means that defying a three-line whip is very serious and has occasionally resulted in an MP being expelled from their own party'! (Oh dear, think of all the income and respectability we would lose!)

We begin to see the real reason for calling these Parliamentary members as 'whips' (whipping MPs, to take certain actions?). My view, and that of a growing number of more knowledgeable authors than I, is that this 'whip' system completely satisfies the definition of 'OLIGARCHY' (the opposite of 'democracy'), i.e., 'communication downwards'. The inescapable conclusion is that a 'political elite' (i.e., the UK Government cabinet) decides the government's policies, and the 'whips' TELL the MPs how to vote when the matter is presented for a full government decision (or else!).

This is fundamentally wrong and offends the whole principal of 'representative democracy'. My remedy as a humble 'man in the street' is simple. Retain the lines of communication but reverse it! In other words, apply the following procedure.

1. As already suggested, individual MPs must (or should) hold regular 'surgeries' for their constituent voters and retain records of their wishes and concerns in a 'data bank'. As part of this function they should discuss matters being considered by government in the near future.

2. Party 'whips' analyse all their MPs monthly data reports and accurately summarise the expressed people's wishes and concerns. That is, if they are willing to do this fairly!

3. 'Whips' then publish detailed quarterly (accurate!) national summaries for the party's 'elite' (i.e., the government's cabinet).
4. The cabinet then prepares draft legislation for the consideration of the whole government.
5. The 'opposition parties' in government produce their own accurate summaries of their returns from MPs for submission, and the government then debates and DECIDES.
6. The parties' returns are then made open and public to help voters make even better decisions at election times.

RESULT The people's collective wisdom is better defined, and the UK's level of democracy is much improved by UPWARD influence.

General elections manifestos

I often read these 'manifestos' at general election times, and like a growing number of ordinary people, I look on them as children's comics! I repeat, yet again, they are no more than critically important 'wordology' selected, by computers for influencing the views of the voter. Next up comes the media who then provides another 'wordology layer' consistent with their own prejudices. When will both the political parties and the media realise, as many of the 'non-voters' realise, that they have been 'SUSSED' because actual actions and their consequences, 'speak louder than words'.

Remedy? The laws to require, in future, some standardisation of FACTUAL information upon the parties' specific intentions in their manifestos for the future, which is capable of being measured against actual results. The areas covered need to be identified by non-political professional disciplines which enables us, ordinary citizens, to make accurate judgements at general election times. Aspects of the quality of people's lives and the environment would feature prominently, as would measures of the 'representativeness' of the people's wishes against actual government actions.

Reducing the 'inequality element' of the UK's regions

Much has been recently (2021/22) written and published about the UK's regional (economic) inequality, insofar as living conditions, public services, investment, employment conditions, with London and the southeast regions being openly and accurately proved, by independent, non-political, professional surveys to be 'far better off'. So what do we get? In comes the 'politic speak' legions again, with a new advertising slogan 'LEVELLING UP'.

We are now told that much more 'investment' will be allocated to the 'poorer' regions in future from public funds, to develop the 'infrastructure' (that sounds a good word, yet few of us really know what it means!), being roads, rail, business investment, education, health etc. My reaction? Since this hidden 'high level of past prejudice' has finally been shown (not from government sources, I suspect) let us, the people in the depressed regions spell out and insist upon ACTUAL 'levelling up'. It's quite simple. A reasonable amount of public funds are allocated to professional, completely non-political accountancy associations and academic economic associations to monitor ACTUAL transfers of public funds out of London and the south east to all of the south west, Midlands, Wales, northern England, Scotland, and Northern Ireland, proportionate, say, to accurate population statistics. Without 'interference' from the 'political sector', easy to understand and provably accurate statistics are published and circulated to all voters by local authorities at least yearly. We have a right to know where OUR money is being used.

Levelling up IS a good policy. So might I also suggest that the same principals are applied to ALL people's INCOMES. For instance, the percentage annual monetary gains of the 'elite classes' nationally, independently assessed, should be much more equal ('LEVEL') to the increased wages of the 'working population', with NO compensating increasing of redundancy levels!

We considered this aspect of 'inequality' in Chapter 8, where we compared average (people's) incomes and living expenses with those for MPs during a recent two-year period. We saw from official statistics yet another gross inequality which results in increased power (and opulence) for the political elite, and the decreased power for the people through reduced living standards and influence in public policy.

What is the remedy? (It gave me so much pleasure in answering this point!) It's simple! By LEVELLING UP of course! How do we do this? By establishing a clear and equal relationship between annual % changes in MPs' PAY with the average % wages for the people. But it does end there! By also establishing a clear and equal relationship between % increases in MPs' expenses (presumably for cost of living raises), with increased allowances to ALL people for cost of living increases! OR by clear and measurable decreased taxation for the working population. Let us not forget two essential points. Firstly, it is the people who actually create the nation's wealth. Secondly, all public funds come from the people. 'Levelling Up', BRING IT ON! BUT with professional, non-political monitoring!

The UK's press and media

Firstly, our press and media MUST remain free to print news reports in whatever manner they choose and upon what subject they choose. Compared to many other nations in the world, the UK's press and media will rank in the top tier. We must accept that their freedom will always contain prejudice to some extent or another. But we should also accept that there is always 'room for improvement' in all activities in a 'civilised world'. Because every nation's press and media can and do influence people's opinions, there has to be improved safeguards. Where a press/media article can be 'reasonably judged to be wholly untrue, considerably distorted/prejudiced, and that the press/media source were fully aware of the real facts', surely to goodness, such an act must be officially condemned. The existing 'control mechanism' (Press Complaints Commission) is, in my view, not strong or independent enough to carry out this task. A new law should be introduced transferring this work to the judiciary, where high court judges, people's juries, prosecuting/defending barristers open to the public, should, in my view, be introduced and again under the watchful eye of public juries. If the existing laws need strengthening, so be it!

Strengthening the 'UNITED' aspect of the 'United Kingdom'

Firstly, let me make it absolutely clear that the 'unification' of our separate nations on these two beautiful islands of ours is an essential, world renowned characteristic, which MUST be preserved, in order to maintain our strengths, independence, security, combined wisdom/abilities AND joint contributions worldwide. BUT I pose the question, how can we strengthen our joint relationships AND preserve independence in governmental actions for each nation, adopting common principals of government, but maintaining and developing the 'UNITED' element as well? As an Englishman (with one proud tablespoon full of Scottish blood in my veins!), I would support Scotland becoming an independent nation ONLY if is supported by a full, fair, properly and independently managed REFERENDUM for all registered Scottish voters giving a clear majority view. Let the Scottish people make the decision, not politicians from each side of the border, who, as we have seen, have their own 'agenda'. If this happens, I feel sure THE PEOPLE of all four separate nations on these two enviable islands of ours would all wish to form similar democratic, independent policies. Then our principals of democratic 'UNITEDNESS' would strengthen. English, Irish, Scottish and Welch would stand together to the envy of less fortunate nations in the world. Firstly, Westminster Parliament would become a world tourist attraction! The 'English' government headquarters would be relocated centrally in England, perhaps Birmingham, Manchester (or even my beloved Nottingham!) Wales would have their government headquarters in Cardiff, Ireland (in both Dublin and Stormont?), Scotland in Edinburgh or Glasgow. The 'United' governments would sit, each year, in each of the nation's capitals, with a 'revolving prime minister' coming from each nation with a strict responsibility for overseeing 'Levelling Up' for all nations. There would be complete 'unification' of all vital government actions for trade, defence, laws, education, health and so on, a bit like the original 'common market' concept. Relations with Europe would be developed and with other democratic nations in the world.

Just to illustrate what I am trying to say. 'Yes' to four separate national governments working together to achieve greater, democratic UNIFICATION. TOGETHER. With our extensive combination of talents and skills, the current UNITED 'KINGDOM' (new word perhaps?) HAS, IN THE PAST, BEEN ENVIED BY THE WORLD. We are far stronger, secure, equal and economically better off, side by side!

The UK monarchy must be retained, BUT with a 'mixed blood element' with 'in line for the throne' roles more equal to the four nations. This example, to the world, is how old monarchy dictatorships of kings and queens, can be 'democratised' to the benefit of nations.

End Conclusion

The whole objective of this book is to persuade readers firstly to accept that declining democracy is a MOST serious crisis for our own nation and the whole world, larger even than the global environmental crisis. If you find it difficult to accept this claim, you can do a very simple test yourself, if you have a computer. Open your 'search' facility, and type in just two words, 'democracy decline'. The first thing you will notice is a whacking big list of books, publications and articles supporting this statement, written by a wide variety of knowledgeable authors. Then, ask yourself, 'would such a wide and extensive collection of such articles and claims all be untrue and unjustified'?

Then comes your most essential, simple task. PLEASE use your vote in whichever way YOU decide, particularly at general elections, after carefully considering which way to vote. Ignore all the various claims, promises and criticisms against other parties, and the 'hints' from the media. Consider yourself, the actual past performance of the government during their terms of office, nationally, locally and your own personal experiences. Read, if you can, a couple of the books I have quoted (or others on the same subject). Support AND USE the argument for a greater use of referendums UPON VITALLY IMPORTANT ISSUES, organised independently. REMEMBER, the 'collective wisdom and will' of the people in all nations is the BEST remedy to make the worlds future BETTER. If the UK's current generation of politicians see a sudden substantial INCREASE in total votes cast, and a serious DECREASE in 'non-voters', they just might start representing OUR needs and wishes.

My conclusion, as an ordinary citizen in a 'part' democratic nation is this.

> Trust and accept the 'collective wisdom' of us the nation's people, after they have been openly provided with all the circumstances of a national matter (both good AND bad), AND have been given a full opportunity to choose, from options upon alternative courses of action, in a fair independently managed referendum, which option YOU wish for.

We do NOT want any more wars unless we are clearly threatened or actually attacked, any more declining people power, any more lies, secrets, any more appalling levels of inequality, any more increasing levels of injustice and reduced public services (which WE pay for). We want, the restoration of higher standards of democracy, justice health, equality, in our nation, and the world generally.

If you choose to ignore all the above warnings, I HAVE to say this to you. 'You get the government you deserve.' The leaders of every nation in the world MUST be brought 'to heel', by the worlds peoples. Choose ways and means that causes no harm to 'ordinary' people and review the nation's LAWS beforehand.

Otherwise, all is lost, and I dread to think how it will all end! (Except for the elite!)

www.ingramcontent.com/pod-product-compliance
Lightning Source LLC
Chambersburg PA
CBHW022351280326
41935CB00007B/149